Math in Focus

Singapore Math
by Marshall Cavendish

Enrichment

Author
Wai-Cheng Low

D1568597

Marshall Cavendish
Education

U.S. Distributor

Houghton
Mifflin
Harcourt

COMMON
CORE

© 2013 Marshall Cavendish International (Singapore) Private Limited
© 2014 Marshall Cavendish Education Pte Ltd
(Formerly known as Marshall Cavendish International (Singapore)
Private Limited)

Published by Marshall Cavendish Education
Times Centre, 1 New Industrial Road, Singapore 536196
Customer Service Hotline: (65) 6213 9444
U.S. Office Tel: (1-914) 332 8888 Fax: (1-914) 332 8882
E-mail: tmesales@mceducation.com
Website: www.mceducation.com

Distributed by
Houghton Mifflin Harcourt
222 Berkeley Street
Boston, MA 02116
Tel: 617-351-5000
Website: www.hmheducation.com/mathinfocus

Cover: © Mike Hill/Getty Images

First published 2013

Math in Focus® Enrichment Course 3
ISBN 978-0-547-57901-6

Printed in Singapore

4 5 6 7 8   1401   17 16 15 14
4500467780   B C D E

Contents

Math in Focus
Singapore Math®
by Marshall Cavendish

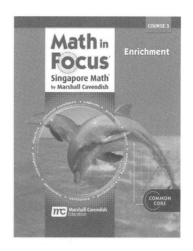

Introducing Math in Focus® Enrichment

Enrichment, written to complement **Math in Focus®: Singapore Math® by Marshall Cavendish**, provides exercises designed for advanced students seeking a challenge beyond the exercises in the Student Books.

Applying Problem-Solving Strategies and Mathematical Practices

These exercises require students to draw on their fundamental mathematical understanding as well as recently acquired concepts and skills, combining problem-solving strategies with good mathematical practices.

Looking For and Using Structure to Solve Problems

Mathematical practices enhanced by trying to solve the unique problems in *Enrichment* exercises include making sense of difficult problems, persevering in solving them, extending mathematical reasoning to new situations, and applying mathematical structures, models and tools to solve problems. Using precise calculations and language during this process leads to clear communication among students and teachers.

Using the Enrichment Exercises

One set of problems is provided for each chapter, including advanced Brain@Work problems. Each problem set should be assigned after the chapter has been completed. *Enrichment* exercises can be assigned while other students are working on the Chapter Review/Test or while the class is working on subsequent chapters.

 Enrichment is also available online and on the Teacher One Stop.

BLANK

CHAPTER

1 Exponents

1. Simplify each expression. Write your answer in exponential notation.

a) $\dfrac{(5^2)^4 \cdot 3^{10} \cdot 5^2}{15^2 \cdot 3^0}$

b) $\dfrac{(7^5 \cdot 7^3)^4 \cdot 7^{-2}}{7^{-7} \cdot 7^{20}}$

c) $\dfrac{(-0.2)^4 \cdot (0.5)^4}{(0.5)^{-5} \cdot (-0.2)^{-5}}$

d) $\left(-\dfrac{6}{35}\right)^3 \cdot \left(-\dfrac{7}{15}\right)^3 \cdot \left(\dfrac{10}{21}\right)^3$

2. Simplify each expression. Write your answer using a positive exponent.

a) $\left(\dfrac{4}{6}a^2b^2\right)^3$

b) $4b^2(3a^2b^5)^{-2}$

c) $\dfrac{81g^{-2} \cdot \left(\dfrac{1}{3}k\right)^{-3}}{27g^{-4}k^{-5}}$

d) $\dfrac{\sqrt{64a^4} \cdot b^4}{64ab^2}$

Solve. Show your work.

3. A cuboid is made up of x number of small cubes with sides 1.2 inches. Given that the volume of the cuboid is 58.8 cubic inches, find x.

4. When an amoeba colony divides, its new population can be determined by multiplying the population before the division by two.

   a) If the initial population of an amoeba colony is 160, what is the population of the colony after it has divided 4 times?

   b) How many divisions need to occur for the population of the amoeba to increase from 160 to 40,960?

5. The thickness of a paper is doubled each time it is folded. The initial thickness of a piece of paper is 0.38 millimeter.

   a) What is the total thickness of the paper after it has been folded 7 times?

   b) If the final thickness of the paper is 12.16 millimeters, how many times has the paper been folded?

6. The following numbers form a sequence: $3, 3^2, 3^3, 3^4, ..., 3^n$.

   a) Find the first ten numbers in the sequence.

   b) If the last number in the sequence is 6,561, what is the value of n?

7. A cylindrical-shaped cup has a height of 7 centimeters and a volume of 112π cubic centimeters. Henry fills the cup completely full of water. He then pours the water from the cup into a cone. If the cone has a radius twice the measure of the cup, what is the height of the cone?

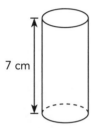 

7 cm

8. Martha bought two identical blocks of clay. Each block of clay has a volume of 64 cubic inches. Martha forms one block of clay into a sphere and she forms the other block of clay into a cube.

a) Find the side length of the cube.

b) Find the radius of the sphere, to the nearest hundredth.

c) Which solid has a greater surface area, the sphere or the cube? Explain how you determined your answer.

9. Find the prime factorization of each number. Write your answers in exponential notation.

   a)   1,008

   b)   864

   c)   Using your answers in **a)** and **b)**, find the greatest common factor of 1,008 and 864. Write your answer in exponential notation.

10. The smallest human cell has a diameter of approximately 10^{-5} meter or 10 micrometers. Assuming that each cell is a perfect sphere, find the volume of 10 trillion (10^{13}) cells.

11. **Brain @ Work**

Geysers are springs of water that are ejected through the Earth's surface at various intervals depending on the temperatures beneath the Earth's volcanic rock. The table shows the approximate frequency of geyser eruptions in Yellowstone National Park.

Name of Geyser	Approximate Frequency of Eruption
Old Faithful	80 minutes
Bead Geyser	32 minutes
Riverside Geyser	375 minutes
Daisy Geyser	175 minutes

a) Find the prime factorization of each value in the approximate frequency of eruption column. Write your answers in exponential notation.

80   32   375   175

b) If the four geysers erupt at the same time at 9:00 A.M., when will the next concurrent eruption take place?

Hint: Find the least common multiple of the approximate eruption frequency values in the table.

12. **Brain @ Work**

On January 1, 2012, Julia deposits $2,500 in her savings account. It will earn 5% interest compounded yearly.

a) If Julia makes no additional deposits and no withdrawals, how much money will be in her account on December 31, 2017?

b) If beginning January 1, 2013, and each year thereafter, Julia deposits $200 into her bank account, how much money will be in her account on December 31, 2017?

c) Given that Julia deposits $2,500 into an account, which type of account will result in a greater balance after 5 years, a 5% yearly compound interest account or a 5% yearly fixed interest account? Explain how you determined your answer.

CHAPTER

Scientific Notation

Solve. Show your work.

1. The table shows the approximate populations of different states in the United States.

State	Population	
	Standard Form	**Scientific Notation**
Florida	19,060,000	
Washington		$6.839 \cdot 10^6$
Tennessee	6,403,000	
New York		$1.945 \cdot 10^7$
Wisconsin	5,712,000	
Minnesota		$5.345 \cdot 10^6$

a) Complete the table.

b) Which pair of states has a greater total population, Florida and Wisconsin or New York and Minnesota?

2. A supersonic aircraft has an average cruising speed of 1,334 miles per hour. It takes approximately 3.5 hours for the aircraft to fly from New York to Paris. It takes a typical commercial aircraft about 8 hours to travel the same distance. Find the average cruising speed of the commercial aircraft. Write your answer in scientific notation. Round the coefficient to the nearest hundredth.

3. A garden snail moves at a speed of 0.002 mile per hour, while a cheetah can reach a top speed of 60 miles per hour. How many times as fast as a cheetah is a snail? Write your answer in the following forms.

    a) As a fraction in simplest form

    b) In scientific notation; round the coefficient to the nearest tenth

    c) As a decimal correct to 3 significant digits

4. The Mariana trench is the deepest part of the world's oceans. The trench has a depth of about 36,000 feet, a length of about 8,300,000 feet, and a mean width of about 230,000 feet.

    a) Write the length, the width, and the depth of the Mariana trench in scientific notation.

    b) Find the approximate volume of the trench. Write your answer in scientific notation. Round the coefficient to the nearest tenth.

5. Bacterial cells are about one-tenth the size of a human cell, with some measuring as small as 0.3 micrometer in length. Express this length in inches. Write your answer in scientific notation.

Note: 1 meter is approximately 39.37 inches.

6. Light travels at a speed of about 670,000,000 miles per hour. It would take someone traveling at the speed of light 10.5 years to reach the nearest solar system to the Earth, Epsilon Eridani. Find the distance, in miles, between the Earth's solar system and that of Epsilon Eridani. Write your answer in scientific notation. Round the coefficient to the nearest hundredth.

Note: 1 year has 365 days.

7. The smallest known insect, a fairyfly, has a body length of only 0.0055 inch while the largest animal in the world, the blue whale, can grow to 110 feet in length. The average height of an American male is 5 feet $9\frac{1}{2}$ inches.

a) How many times as large as the fairyfly is the height of the average American male? Write your answer in scientific notation. Round the coefficient to the nearest tenth.

b) How many times as large as the blue whale is the height of the average American male? Write your answer in scientific notation. Round the coefficient to the nearest tenth.

8. The United States has a labor force of approximately $1.4 \cdot 10^8$ people. The table shows the distribution of the labor force among five categories of occupations.

Categories	Distribution of U.S. Labor Force
Farming, forestry, and fishing	0.01
Manufacturing, extraction, transportation, and crafts	0.20
Managerial, professional, and technical	0.37
Sales and office	0.24
Other services	0.18

a) Approximately how many people work in the 'Sales and office' category? Write your answer in scientific notation.

b) Find the difference between the number of people working in the 'Farming, forestry, and fishing' category and the number of people working in the 'Managerial, professional, and technical' category. Write your answer in scientific notation.

9. The H1N1 influenza virus measures 120 nanometer. One nanometer is approximately equal to $3.9 \cdot 10^{-8}$ inch.

a) Find the length of the H1N1 virus in inches. Write your answer in scientific notation.

b) Standard optical microscopes can only see objects with lengths to $3.917 \cdot 10^{-5}$ inch. Find how many times as large as its actual size the virus would be seen under a standard optical microscope. Round your answer to the nearest hundredth.

10. An electron has a mass of about $9.11 \cdot 10^{-31}$ kilogram. Its mass is about $\dfrac{1}{1,836}$ that of a proton, and about $\dfrac{1}{1,838}$ that of a neutron. Find the approximate mass of a neutron and a proton. Write your answer in scientific notation. Round the coefficient to the nearest thousandth.

a) A neutron

b) A proton

11. Brain @ Work

Daniel wants to build a model of the solar system. He uses 3 feet to represent 1 Astronomical Unit (AU). One Astronomical Unit is approximately 93,000,000 miles, which is the approximate average distance from the Earth to the Sun.

a) Write the average distance from the Earth to the Sun in scientific notation.

b) The distance from the Earth to the moon is approximately 240,000 miles. What would this distance be in Daniel's model? Write your answer in scientific notation. Round the coefficient to the nearest tenth.

c) Since the Earth and Jupiter both have elliptical (noncircular) orbits, the distance from the Earth to Jupiter varies. In Daniel's model, he can position Jupiter anywhere between 12.6 feet and 18.6 feet from the Earth. What is the range of the actual distance from the Earth to Jupiter, in miles? Write your answer in scientific notation.

12. Brain @ Work

The table shows the number of Internet users from 2005 to 2010.

Year	Number of Internet Users (in millions)
2005	1,018
2006	1,093
2007	1,262
2008	1,400
2009	1,530
2010	1,650

a) Find the difference between the number of Internet users in 2006 and in 2007. Write your answer in scientific notation.

b) Find the average number of Internet users from 2008 through 2010. Write your answer in scientific notation. Round the coefficient to the nearest tenth.

c) How many times as many Internet users were there in 2010 than in 2005? Round your answer to the nearest tenth.

Name: _____ Date: _____

 Algebraic Linear Equations

Solve. Show your work.

1. The measure of one angle of a triangle is 9.2° greater than the measure of the smallest angle. The measure of the third angle is 30.8° less than 2.5 times the measure of the smallest angle. Find the measures of the three angles.

2. Two yachts are 39 miles apart. As they travel towards each other, they pass each other after $\frac{1}{3}$ hour. Given one yacht travels 6 miles per hour faster than the other, find the speeds of both yachts.

3. Margaret buys a roll of ribbon from a shop. She cuts the ribbon into three pieces. The ratio of the length of the shortest piece to the length of the longest is 2 : 3. The third piece is $1\frac{3}{4}$ feet shorter than the longest piece.

   a) If the total length of the three ribbons is $\left(\frac{8}{3}x - \frac{7}{4}\right)$ feet, can Margaret find the length of each piece of ribbon? Explain.

   b) After reading the label on the ribbon roll package, Margaret finds that the total length of the ribbon is $22\frac{1}{4}$ feet long. Can she find the length of each piece of ribbon using this measure? If so, how long is each piece of ribbon?

4. James rides his bicycle every Sunday morning. First, he pedals uphill at a speed of 4 miles per hour. Then he rides downhill at a speed of 6 miles per hour. He covers a distance of 18 miles in 4 hours.

    a) Write a linear equation for the distance pedaled, d miles.

    b) For how many miles does he travel downhill?

    c) What is the difference in time spent pedaling uphill versus riding downhill?

5. Casey can install a fountain in a school garden in 20 hours. Samuel can install a similar fountain in the same school garden in 30 hours. If they work together, they would take a total of t hours to install the fountain.

a) What fraction of the fountain can each of them install in one hour?

b) Write an algebraic expression in terms of t for the fraction of the fountain they can install together in one hour.

c) Write an equation for t. Solve for t to find the total number of hours they would take to install the fountain if they work together.

6. The ratio of the perimeter of triangle *PQR* to the perimeter of rectangle
ABCD is 5 : 9.

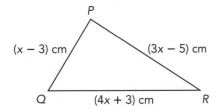 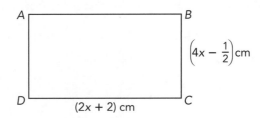

a) Write algebraic expressions for the perimeters of triangle *PQR* and
rectangle *ABCD*.

b) Write a linear equation using the algebraic expressions for the
perimeters in **a)**. Then solve for *x*.

c) Find the area of rectangle *ABCD*.

7. The following number sequence is generated from a pattern of squares formed using paper clips.

Diagram 1   **Diagram 2**   **Diagram 3**   **Diagram 4**

a) Write a linear equation for the number of paper clips used in each diagram, m, in terms of the number of squares in each diagram, n.

b) Use the equation in **a)** to complete the table of values below.

Number of Squares (n)	1	2	3	4	5	...	10
Number of Paper Clips (m)							

c) Find the number of paper clips needed to form 40 squares.

d) If Jimmy has 80 paper clips, how many squares can he form? Will there be any leftover paper clips?

8. Mrs. Davidson bought some flour at w per pound. She also bought some ground coffee, which cost six times the price per pound of the flour. She paid $12.60 for the flour and $27 for the ground coffee.

a) Write algebraic expressions for the masses of flour and coffee purchased.

b) If the total mass of flour and ground coffee purchased was 9.5 pounds, write a linear equation for the total mass of wheat flour and coffee powder purchased.

c) Solve for w to find the price per pound of the flour and the price per pound of the ground coffee.

9. The volume of a square pyramid is represented by $V = \frac{1}{3}Bh$, where B is the area of the square base and h is the height of the pyramid.

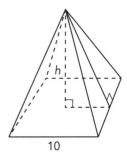

10

a) Express h in terms of V and B.

b) Find the height of the pyramid if its volume is 400 cubic centimeters and the length of the square base is 10 centimeters.

c) Find the surface area of the pyramid.

10. **Brain @ Work**

In the diagram, MNPR is a square and MQS is an isosceles triangle. The length of the side of square MNPR is $(3x - 2)$ inches. The length of $\overline{QR}$ is $\left(\dfrac{8}{x + 1}\right)$ inches. If the area of triangle MQS is 14 square inches, find the area of MNPQ.

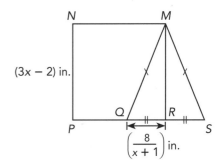

Name: _____   Date: _____

11. Brain @ Work

Melody is paid $M per week. She earns a weekly flat wage of $80 plus an additional $0.15 for each of the n customers she advises. Her salary, M, in terms of the number of customers she advises, n, is represented by $M = 80 + \frac{15n}{100}$.

a) Find the salary she receives for advising 360 customers for 4 consecutive weeks.

b) Melody received $140 at the end of a certain week. How many customers did she advise that week?

c) Melody's employer decides to decrease her basic wage to $65 and increase her salary per customer advised to $0.21. Write a linear equation to represent her new salary, M, in terms of the number of customers she advises, n.

d) Find the number of customers she would have to advise in one week in order for her to receive the same amount of money before the decrease in basic wage.

CHAPTER

Lines and Linear Equations

Solve. Show your work.

1. Line L_1 has the equation $x = -\dfrac{1}{4}y - 3$ and line L_2 has the equation $\dfrac{x}{3} + \dfrac{y}{2} = 4$.
   Find an equation of a line parallel to L_1 that has the same y-intercept as L_2.

2. A line with slope $-\dfrac{1}{2}$ passes through point $Q\,(6, 7)$. Does point $S\,(2, 5)$ lie on this line?

3. There were 900 students enrolled in a high school in 2009 and 1,500 students enrolled in the same high school in 2012. The student enrollment of the high school, P, has increased at a constant rate each year, t, since 2009.

   a) Translate the verbal description into two pair of points in the form (t, P).

   b) Find the slope of the line passing through the pair of points in **a)** and explain what information it gives about the situation.

   c) Write an equation that relates the high school's student enrollment, P, to the number of years since 2009, t.

   d) Predict the high school's student enrollment in 2017.

4. Michael starts from Town A at 9:00 A.M. and bikes towards Town B at a
constant speed of 16 miles per hour. Town A and Town B are 48 miles apart.
George follows the same route as Michael but starts at 10:00 A.M. and drives
at a constant speed of 48 miles per hour.

a) Graph, on the same axes, the distance traveled by Michael and George.
Use 1 unit on the horizontal axis to represent 0.5 hour for the *x* interval
from 0 to 3.0, and 1 unit on the vertical axis to represent 8 miles for the
y interval from 0 to 48.

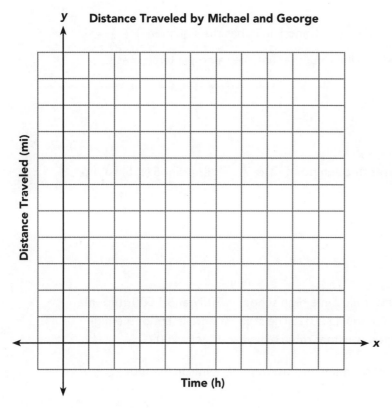

b) At what distance and at what time will George pass Michael?

c) At what time must Michael leave if he wants to reach Town B at the
same time as George?

5. The table shows the cost of strawberries at two supermarkets.

Weight of Strawberries (x pounds)	Cost at Supermarket A (y dollars)	Cost at Supermarket B (y dollars)
1	2.00	1.50
2	4.00	3.00
3	6.00	4.50

a) Graph the relationship between cost and weight of strawberries for each supermarket. Use 2 units on the horizontal axis to represent 1 pound for the x interval from 0 to 3. Use 1 unit on the vertical axis to represent $0.50 for the y interval from 0 to 6.

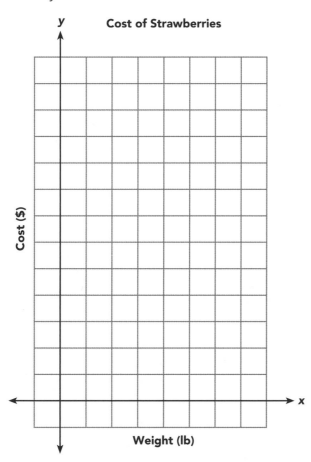

b) Which supermarket has the least expensive strawberries per pound? Explain how you determined your answer.

6. Candles A, B, and C are of the same length but have different thickness. The graph below shows the changes in the length, *y* centimeters, of the candles when burning for *t* hours.

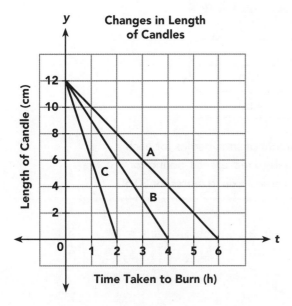

a) Identify the *y*-intercept of the graph. What does it represent?

b) Write the equations of the three graphs in the form $y = mx + b$.

c) Candle A and Candle B were lit at the same time. At *t* hours, Jesse observed that Candle A was twice as long as Candle B. How long before *t* hours were the 2 candles lit?

7. Alvin and Megan both live in Town A. They attended a conference in Town B, which is 180 miles from Town A. After the conference, they began driving back to Town A at the same time but were driving at different speeds. Alvin was traveling at a speed of 60 miles per hour while Megan was traveling at a speed of 45 miles per hour.

a) Write the linear equations that represent Alvin's and Megan's distance, y miles, from Town A x hours after they start driving.

b) Graph on the same axes, Megan and Alvin's return trip from Town B as it relates to distance, y miles, and time, x hours. Use 2 units on the horizontal axis to represent 1 hour for the x interval from 0 to 4 and 1 unit on the vertical axis to represent 30 miles for the y interval from 0 to 180.

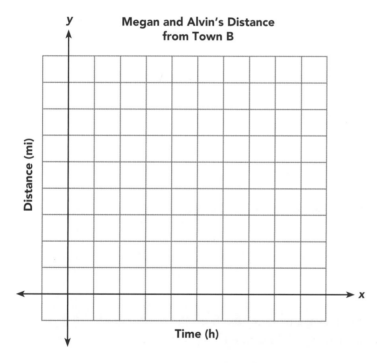

Megan and Alvin's Distance from Town B

Distance (mi)

Time (h)

c) Who would reach Town A first? How do you know?

d) How much earlier would the second person have to leave Town B for both of them to arrive at the same time?

8. Susan plans to buy a hand-painted porcelain vase from a craft studio. She is aware that the total price of the vase consists of the porcelain vase plus the artist's hourly painting fee. The graph shows the price of a vase offered by Studio A. Studio B sells an unpainted vase for $18 with a two-hour painting fee of $22.

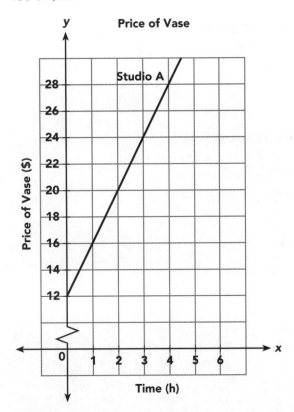

a) Find the price of the unpainted porcelain vase at Studio A.

b) Graph the cost of the porcelain vase from Studio B on the coordinate plane above. Then find the artist's painting rate at each studio.

c) In what situation will it be cheaper to buy a vase from Studio A than Studio B?

9. Rita and Thomas both drive to Town R to attend a meeting. Rita starts her journey from Town P whereas Thomas starts his journey from Town Q. Town Q is between Town P and Town R, and is 40 miles away from Town P. They begin their journey at the same time but drive at different speeds. Thomas arrives at Town R one hour later than Rita.

The graph shows the distance, y miles, from Town P, x hours after Rita starts her journey.

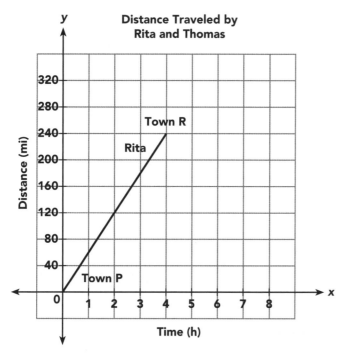

a) How far away is Town R from Town P?

b) On the coordinate plane above, draw a line to represent Thomas' journey.

c) Find the slope of each graph, and explain what information it gives about the situation.

d) Write an equation to represent the distance, y miles, from Town P, after x hours for both Rita and Thomas.

10. The table below shows the boiling point of water at various altitudes.

Altitude (x feet)	0	1,000	2,000
Boiling Point (y°F)	212.0	210.2	208.4

a) Graph the relationship between the boiling point of water and altitude.
Use 2 units on the horizontal axis to represent 1,000 feet for the x interval
from 0 to 2,000. Use 1 unit on the vertical axis to represent 0.6°F for the
y interval from 208.4 to 212.0.

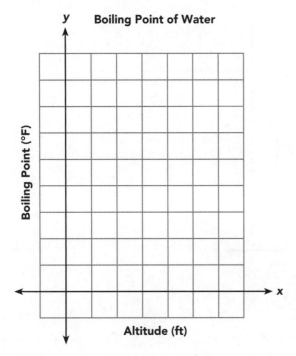

b) Identify the y-intercept of the graph and explain what information it gives
about the situation.

c) What is the rate of change of the boiling point of water per 500 feet?

d) Predict the boiling point of water at an altitude of 7,500 feet.

11. **Brain @ Work**

A group of students are planning to organize a concert to raise funds for building a new stadium. The goal is to sell $1,800 worth of tickets.

a) They plan to charge x for an adult ticket and y for a student ticket. If 100 adults and 200 students are predicted to attend, write a linear equation to represent this situation.

b) Graph the linear equation from **a)** in the following grid. Use 1 unit on the horizontal axis to represent $4 for the x interval from 0 to 24. Use 1 unit on the vertical axis to represent $2 for the y interval from 0 to 12.

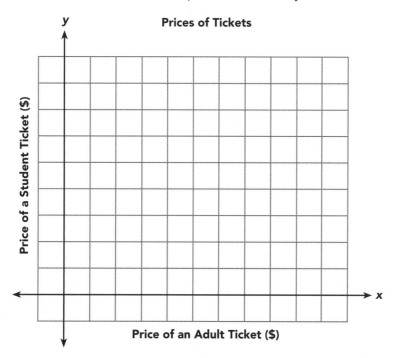

c) Identify the y-intercept of the graph and explain what it represents in this situation.

d) Find the x-intercept of the graph and explain what it represents in this situation.

e) If students cannot afford to pay more than $4 for a ticket, what can you say about the price of an adult ticket?

12. **Brain @ Work**

A factory manufactures 500 uniforms a week and sells them for $20 each. The total cost of manufacturing 500 uniforms per week involves a fixed cost and a variable cost. The graph shows the amount of money involved in producing *n* shirts.

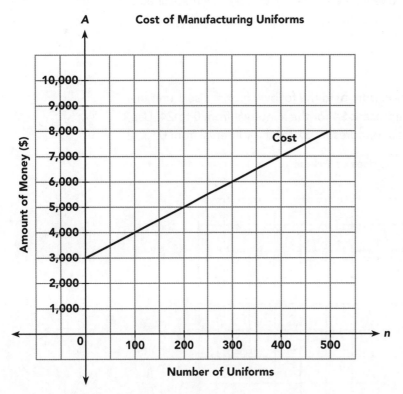

a) Identify the *y*-intercept of the graph and explain what information it gives about the situation.

b) Find the slope of the graph and explain what information it gives about the situation.

c) On the coordinate grid above, draw a line to represent the income earned for *n* shirts.

d) If the factory sells 200 shirts, will they make a profit or a loss? Explain your reasoning.

e) How many shirts must the factory sell to break even? Explain.

CHAPTER

Systems of Linear Equations

Solve each system of linear equations.

1. $\dfrac{x}{3} + \dfrac{y}{2} = 4$

   $\dfrac{2x}{3} - \dfrac{y}{6} = 1$

2. $0.8x - 3y = -6$

   $1.2x + 0.5y = 3$

Solve. Show your work.

3. Five years ago, Mrs. Merlin was 8 times as old as her son, Josh. The sum of their present ages is 46. If Mr. Merlin is one year older than Mrs. Merlin, how old will Mr. Merlin be two years from now?

4. Steve and Ben have some money in their wallets. If Steve gives Ben $3, Ben will have twice as much as Steve. If Ben gives Steve $7, the amount Ben has will be one-third that of Steve's. How much money do Steve and Ben each have in their wallets?

5. Mr. and Mrs. Johnson and their eight-year-old son visited a museum. They paid a total of $16.50 for their museum admission tickets. A group of tourists consisting of 17 adults and 8 children paid $138 for their admission tickets to the same musuem.

   a)   What is the price of an adult museum ticket? What is the price of a child museum ticket?

   b)   What is the total cost of museum tickets for 3 adults and 12 children?

6. Two cars leave town at the same time and travel in opposite directions. The average rate of speed of one car is 15 miles per hour faster than the average rate of speed of the other car. The cars are 375 miles apart after three hours. Find the average rate of speed of the two cars.

7. James and George are both cycling on the same road. They are currently 21 miles apart. If the two cyclists bike towards each other, they will pass each other in 36 minutes. If they cycle in the same direction, James will pass George in 7 hours. Find the average rate of speed, in miles per hour, of both cyclists.

8. One-fifth of the sum of the numerator and the denominator of a particular fraction is 8. If the numerator of a fraction is subtracted from 22, the original fraction becomes $\frac{1}{3}$. What is the original fraction?

9. A necklace made of silver and gold has a mass of 92.5 grams. The volume of the necklace is 8 cubic centimeters. The density of gold is about 19 grams per cubic centimeter and the density of silver is about 10.5 grams per cubic centimeter. Find what percent of the necklace is made of silver.

Note: Mass = Density · Volume

10. A chemist combines a 30% Acid solution A and an 80% Acid solution B to form a 70% acid solution. If the chemist makes 150 milliliters of the 70% acid solution, how much of Solution A and Solution B did he use?

11. A fitness club has two payment options, one for club members and one for nonclub members. Members pay a one-time registration fee of $12 plus $8 per gym visit. Nonclub members pay $10 per gym visit.

    a) Write a system of linear equations for the cost, C, of the two payment options in terms of the number of visits, n.

    b) Solve the system of linear equations graphically.

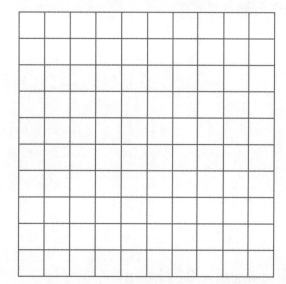

    c) After how many gym visits is the payment for the member option more beneficial than the payment for the nonclub member option?

12. The cost of 40 party hats and 10 balloons is $13.20. The cost of 20 party hats and 5 balloons is $6.60.

a) Write a system of linear equations to find the cost of a party hat, h, and a balloon, b.

b) Can the system of equations in a) be used to find the cost of one party hat and one balloon? Explain your reasoning.

c) If 8 party hats and 4 balloons cost $2.88, how can this information be used to determine the cost of one party hat and one balloon? Explain.

13. **Brain @ Work**

The positions of the digits of a certain two-digit number are swapped. The difference between the original two-digit number and the new two-digit number is 54. The ones digit of the original number is three more than twice the tens digit. What is the original two-digit number?

14. Brain @ Work

David plans to donate any money earned from selling T-shirts to a charity. The table shows the number of T-shirts David wants to sell.

Size	Quantity
Small	x
Medium	y
Large	z

The table shows two options for pricing the T-shirts.

	Price of T-Shirts	Total Amount Earned
Option A	Small: $4 Medium: $6 Large: $10	$620
Option B	Small: $6 Medium: $8 Large: $10	$740

a) Find two possible sets of solutions for x, y, and z.

b) Are your answers for **a)** the only possible solutions? Explain your reasoning.

Name: _____   Date: _____

CHAPTER

6 Functions

Solve. Show your work.

1. A sequence of dots is shown in the diagram.

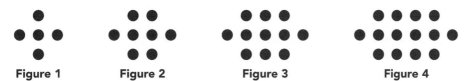

| Figure 1 | Figure 2 | Figure 3 | Figure 4 |

a) Construct an input-output table for the sequence. Use the figure number *n*, as the input and the number of dots, *D*, as the output.

b) Identify the type of relation between the figure number and the number of dots in a figure.

c) Tell whether the relation in **a)** is a function. Explain if the relation is a function and represent it with an algebraic equation.

2. A sporting goods store buys baseball caps in bulk quantities and resells the caps for a profit. The store purchased a bulk quantity of baseball cap for $300. The store's total profit on the baseball caps, p dollars, is a function of the number of baseball caps, n, the store sells.

a) Given that the sporting goods store sells the baseball caps for $7.50 each, write an algebraic equation to represent the profit as a function of the number of baseball caps sold.

b) In a function, the domain is the set of input values and the range is the set of output values. Referring to the equation you wrote in **a)** what do the domain and range represent?

c) Find the range of the function when the domain is {0, 20, 30, 40, 50}. What information can you draw from the values of the range?

3. A submarine was cruising at 1,200 feet below sea level. It then ascended at a rate of 15 feet per minute.

a) Write an algebraic equation to represent the depth of the submarine D in feet after it ascends for t minutes.

b) Construct a table of t and D values for the function in **a)**. Use $t = 0, 10, 20, 30, 40,$ and 50.

c) Use the table of values in **b)** to draw a graph that represents the function. Use 2 units on the horizontal axis to represent 10 minutes for the *t* interval from 0 to 50, and 2 units on the vertical axis to represent −200 feet for the *D* interval from 0 to −1,200.

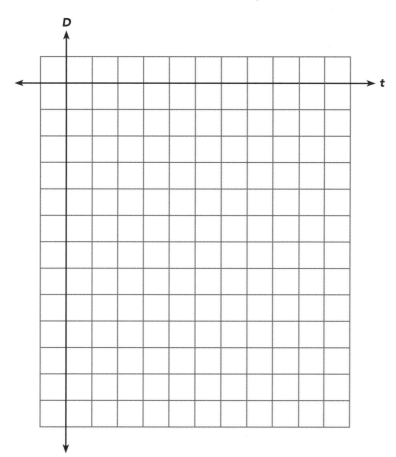

d) If the submarine continues to ascend at the same rate, determine how long it will take to reach the surface of the water. Explain how you determined your answer.

4. Trey needs to rent a car for one day. The rental company offers two plans. Both plans involve paying a fixed amount and then paying an additional charge per mile driven. For each plan, the cost of driving the car, y dollars, is a function of the number of miles traveled. The graph shows the car rental cost for Plan A. Plan B offers a fixed payment of $30 plus 25¢ a mile.

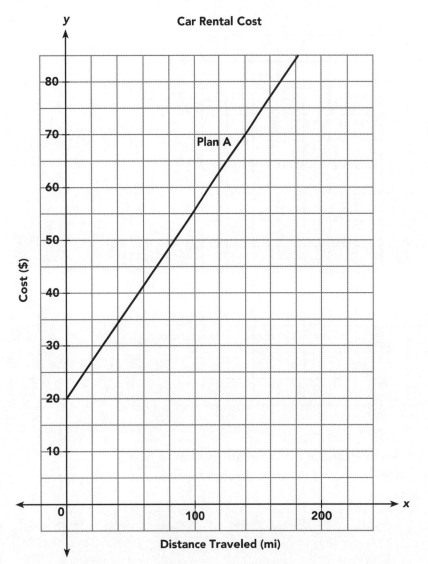

Car Rental Cost

a) Write an algebraic equation to represent the function for Plan B.

b) Graph the linear function for Plan B on the same coordinate plane as Plan A.

© Marshall Cavendish International (Singapore) Private Limited.

c) Use a verbal description to compare the two functions. Describe a scenario that would benefit Trey to rent the car using Plan A. Then describe a scenario that would benefit Trey using Plan B.

d) Describe a situation where either rental plan results in the same total cost.

5. The wholesale price, P dollars, for a case of CD boxes is a function of the manufacturing cost, x dollars, per box. There are 12 boxes per case and the manufacturer includes a $5 markup.

a) Write an algebraic equation for the wholesale price, P dollars, in terms of the manufacturing cost x dollars, per box.

b) The retail price Q includes a 40% markup on the wholesale price. So, $Q = P + 0.4P$. Write a function that expresses the retail price of a case of 12 CD boxes in terms of x.

c) Find the retail price of a case of 12 CD boxes that costs $0.05 per box to manufacture.

6. A spring has an initial length of 60 centimeters. The length of the spring increases when a weight is attached to it. The length of the stretched spring, *y* centimeters, is a function of the weight attached to it, *x* kilograms. The table shows the lengths of the spring, *y* centimeters, for different weights, *x* kilograms.

Weight (*x* kilograms)	0	10	15	20
Length of Spring (*y* centimeters)	60	62	63	64

a) Graph the function. Use 2 units on the horizontal axis to represent 10 kilograms for the *x* interval from 0 to 20, and 2 units on the vertical axis to represent 2 centimeters for the *y* interval from 60 to 64.

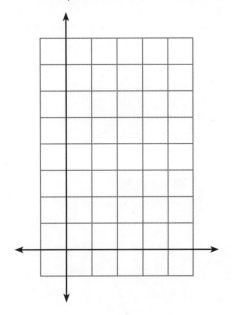

b) Find the vertical intercept and the slope of the graph and explain what information it gives about the situation.

c) Write down an algebraic equation to represent the function.

d) Determine the length of the spring when a 40-kilogram weight is attached to it.

© Marshall Cavendish International (Singapore) Private Limited.

7. A restaurant has some fixed operation costs and some operation costs that vary with the number of patrons. The monthly operating costs C, is a function of the number of monthly patrons, n. If the restaurant has 3,000 patrons in one month, the monthly operating costs are $1,400. If the restaurant has 1,000 patrons in one month, the operating costs are $600.

a) Translate the verbal description into two ordered pairs in the form (input n, output C) for the function.

b) Graph the function. Use 2 units on the horizontal axis to represent $500 for the x interval from 0 to 3,000, and 2 units on the vertical axis to represent 200 patrons for the y interval from 200 to 1,400.

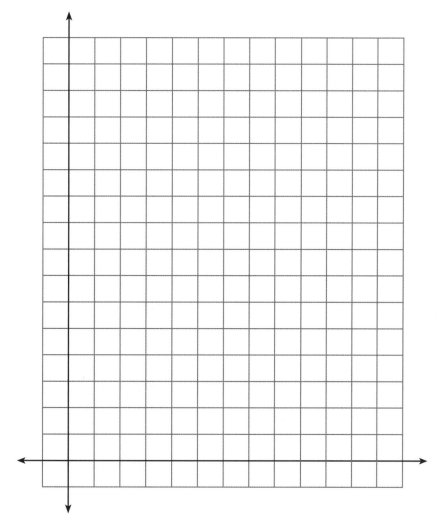

c) Write an algebraic equation for the function.

d) Predict the monthly operating costs for this restaurant if there are only 250 monthly patrons.

8. Patricia has $60. She is spending it at a rate of $2 a week. Her sister, Veronica, has $40 and is adding to her savings at a rate of $3 a week. The amount of money, y, that each sister will have after x weeks is a linear function.

    a) Write two algebraic equations to represent the respective linear functions of the two sisters.

    b) Use a verbal description to compare the two functions.

    c) Graph the two functions on the same coordinate plane. Use 1 unit on the horizontal axis to represent 1 week for the x interval from 0 to 10, and 2 units on the vertical axis to represent $10 for the y interval from 0 to 70.

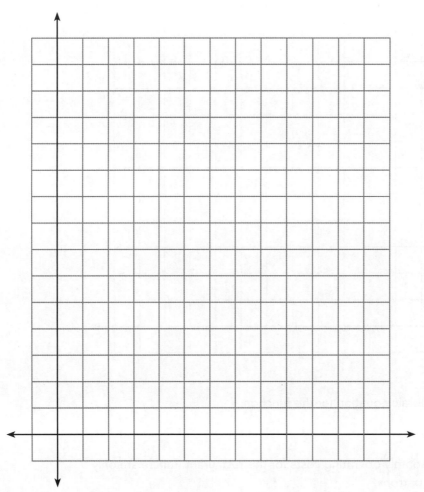

d) Use the graphs to estimate when the two sisters will have the same amount of money.

9. The table shows the fines imposed on an overdue library book.

Number of Days Overdue (x)	1	2	3	4	5
Amount of Fine (y cents)	5	10	15	20	25

Graph the relationship between x and y. Use 2 units on the horizontal axis to represent 1 day for the x interval from 0 to 5, and 2 units on the vertical axis to represent 5 cents for the y interval from 0 to 25. Determine if the points on the graph should be connected. Then, identify the type of relation represented and explain if this relation represents a function.

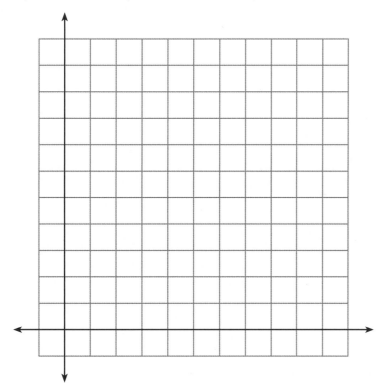

10. You drive your car for 2 hours at a constant speed of 50 miles per hour. You stop at a rest area for 4 hours and then resume driving at a constant speed of 50 miles per hour. Graph the relationship between x and y. Use 1 unit on the horizontal axis to represent 1 hour for the x interval from 0 to 8, and 2 units on the vertical axis to represent 20 miles for the y interval from 0 to 100. Determine if the points on the graph should be connected. Then, identify the type of relation represented and explain if this relation represents a function.

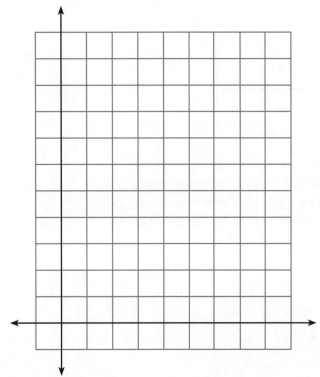

11. The table shows the parking rates charged by a parking garage. Graph the relationship between x and y. Use 2 units on the horizontal axis to represent 2 hours for the x interval from 0 to 8, and 2 units on the vertical axis to represent $3 for the y interval from 0 to 12. Then, identify the type of relation represented and explain if this relation represents a function.

Number of Hours Parked (x hours)	Cost of Parking (y dollars)
$0 < x \leq 2$	3
$2 < x \leq 4$	6
$4 < x \leq 6$	9
$6 < x \leq 8$	12

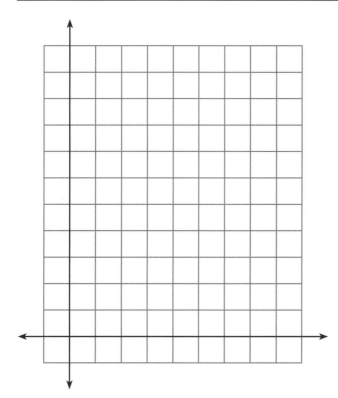

12. The perimeter and the area of a square are related to the side length of the square.

a) Complete the table for the perimeter, P, and the area, A, of a square with a side length of x inches.

Length of Side (x inches)	1	$1\frac{1}{2}$	2	$2\frac{1}{2}$	3
Perimeter (P inches)	4				
Area (A square inches)	1				

b) Graph the function representing the perimeter, P, of the square in terms of its length x. Use 2 units on the horizontal axis to represent 1 inch for the x interval from 0 to 5, and 2 units on the vertical axis to represent 2 inches for the y interval from 0 to 16.

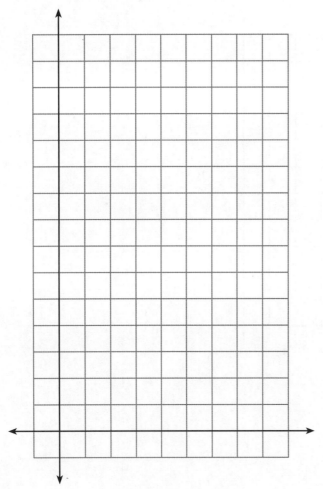

© Marshall Cavendish International (Singapore) Private Limited.

c) Graph the function representing the area *A* of the square in terms of its length *x*. Use 2 units on the horizontal axis to represent 1 inch for the *x* interval from 0 to 5, and 2 units on the vertical axis to represent 2 inches for the *y* interval from 0 to 16.

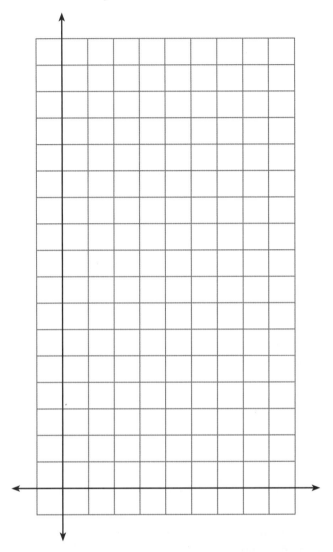

d) Identify each function as linear or nonlinear. Explain.

13. **Brain @ Work**

An electrical home supply store offers a $150 rebate and a 20% discount off of the price of any the electrical appliance.

a) Write an algebraic equation to represent the cost after rebate function $C(x)$, after receiving only the rebate, for an electrical appliance that costs x dollars.

b) Write an algebraic equation to represent the discounted price function $D(x)$, after only applying the discount, for an electrical appliance that costs x dollars.

c) The composition of two functions is a way to combine two functions by successive applications of the functions in a specific order. Write a composite function for the final cost of an electrical appliance, assuming the discount first is applied to the price.

d) Write a composite function for the final cost of an electrical appliance, assuming the rebate is applied to the price first.

e) A customer purchases a $2,000 electrical appliance. Which function is most advantageous to the customer? Explain.

14. **Brain @ Work**

The amount of kinetic energy (energy of motion) of a moving body, E joules, varies directly as the square of its velocity, v meters per second.

a) Assume that the kinetic energy of a person walking at a rate of 2 meters per second is 140 joules. Find the constant of proportionality. Write down an equation for the function.

b) Use the equation in **a)** to find the kinetic energy if the person is running at 5 meters per second.

c) Express v in terms of E.

CHAPTER

The Pythagorean Theorem

Solve. Show your work. Round your answers to the nearest tenth.

1. In the diagram, $EF = 15.3$ in., $FC = 20$ in., $AC = 10$ in., $DF = 19.6$ in., and $BCED$ is a rectangle. Find the length of $\overline{AD}$.

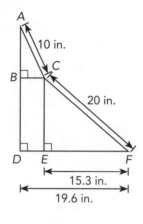

2. The following diagrams show the plans of Mr. Jackson's and Mr. Smith's lawns, with the shaded area representing each lawn. Mr. Jackson and Mr. Smith both want to build a fence around their lawns.

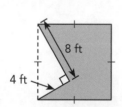

Mr. Jackson's lawn

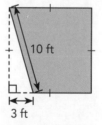

Mr. Smith's lawn

   a) Who has a greater area of lawn?

   b) Find the length of the fences required for each lawn. Which lawn requires the least amount of linear fencing?

3. Pedro wants to buy triangular-shaped wings for his model airplane. The table shows the dimensions of four types of triangular-shaped model airplane wings sold by a particular hobby store.

Wing Options	Leg 1 (cm)	Leg 2 (cm)	Hypotenuse (cm)
A	15	36	39
B	8	25	27
C	9	40	41
D	33	56	60

Pedro is only considering wing options that are in the shape of a right triangle. Which option(s), if any, is Pedro considering?

4. A textbook has a length of 6 inches, a height of y inches, and a width of x inches. If the length of the diagonal of the front cover is 8 inches, and the length of the diagonal of the width is 7 inches, find the values of x and y.

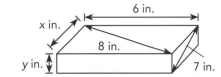

5. Jack starts at point A and runs up a hill at a rate of 8 miles per hour to point C. At the same time, Jill starts at point B and runs up a hill at a rate of 10 miles per hour to point C. Which runner will reach point C first? Explain how you determined your answer.

Note: 1 mile = 5,280 feet

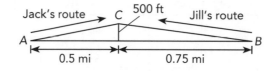

6. A park ranger uses a coordinate grid to plot the locations of campsites in a forest. The location of Campsite A is at point (−6, 3) while the location of Campsite B is at point (4, 7). Given that the ranger station is located at point (2, 1), which campsite is closest to the ranger station?

7. Two cars started from the same location. The red car traveled due north and the blue car traveled due east at a speed twice as fast as the red car. Find the speed of each car in miles per hour if they are 150 miles apart after two hours.

Solve. Show your work. Use 3.14 as an approximation for π. Round your answer to the nearest tenth.

8. Paul is building a model space shuttle using a cone, a cylinder, and a hemisphere. Find the volume of the model space shuttle.

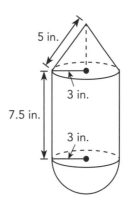

9. A cone has a slant height of 7.8 inches and a radius of 4.5 inches. Kenny cuts off the top of the cone to make a wedge, as shown. Given that the removed top is a smaller cone with a slant height of 3 inches and a radius of 1.5 inches, find the volume of the wedge.

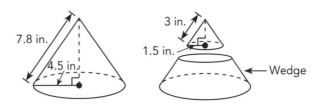

10. A toy is made up of a cylinder and a cone. The volume of the toy
is 4.92 cubic inches. Find the values of x and y.

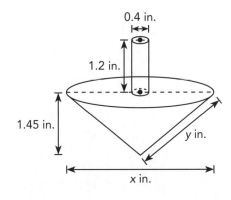

11. Brain @ Work

Martha wants to make a flag banner for a carnival. Each flag in the banner is
an isosceles triangle. How many flags can she make from a rectangular piece
of 5 feet by 5 feet fabric?

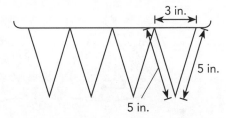

12. **Brain @ Work**

Greek mathematician, Theodorus of Cyrene, created the Wheel of Theodorus to explore the relationship between the hypotenuses of right triangles. Use the Wheel of Theodorus to answer the following questions.

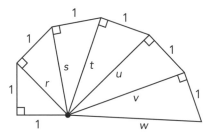

Wheel of Theodorus

a)   Given that the first right triangle has a base and height of 1 unit, find the lengths of the hypotenuses r, s, t, and u.

b)   Find a pattern to relate the lengths of r, s, t, and u. Then predict the length of hypotenuses v and w.

CHAPTER

Geometric Transformations

Solve. Show your work.

1. Richard is located at point (3, 4). A treasure is located at point (−4, −4). Describe the translation that will lead him to the treasure, both in words and algebraically.

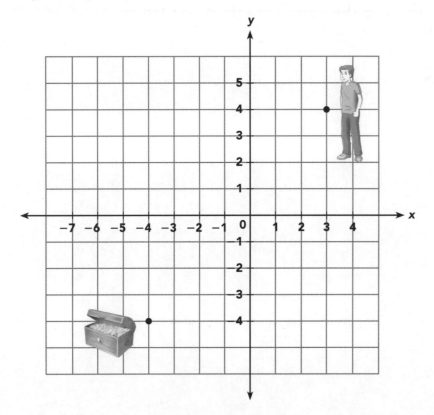

2. Calvin takes a picture with his cell phone camera. On the cell phone screen, the photo measures 2.4 inches by 1.8 inches. When he uploads the photo onto his computer, the image that appears on his computer screen measures 6 inches by 4.5 inches. When he prints the photo on photo paper, the image displayed on the computer screen has been reduced by a scale factor of $-\frac{1}{3}$.

   a) Find the scale factor of dilation when the photo from Calvin's screen is displayed on the computer screen.

   b) What are the dimensions of the printed photo?

3. Shanti is making a patchwork quilt. Each piece of fabric has a black star on it. She uses the grid below to plan the locations of different fabric squares.

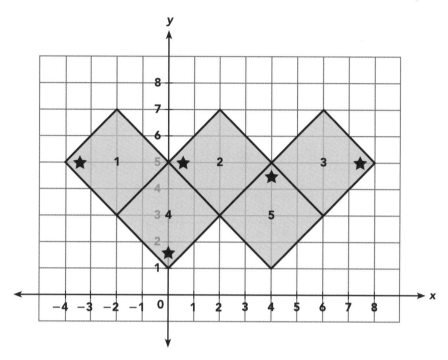

a) What transformation maps square 1 onto square 2?

b) What transformation maps square 2 onto square 3?

c) What transformation maps square 1 onto square 5?

© Marshall Cavendish International (Singapore) Private Limited.

4. The figure shows a clock face with a minute hand and an hour hand.

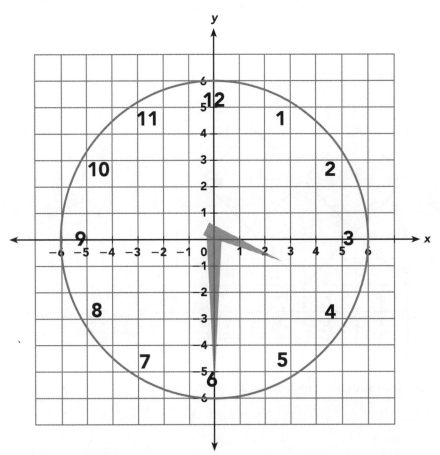

a) Describe the transformation that maps the hour hand when the time changes from 12:00 P.M. to 3:30 P.M.

b) What are the coordinates of the tip of the minute hand at 12:45 P.M.?

c) State the angle of rotation by the minute hand when the time changes from 1:00 P.M. to 2:30 P.M.

Note: Consider 360° as a complete revolution.

© Marshall Cavendish International (Singapore) Private Limited.

5. A toy car represented as *ABCD* is drawn on the coordinate plane.

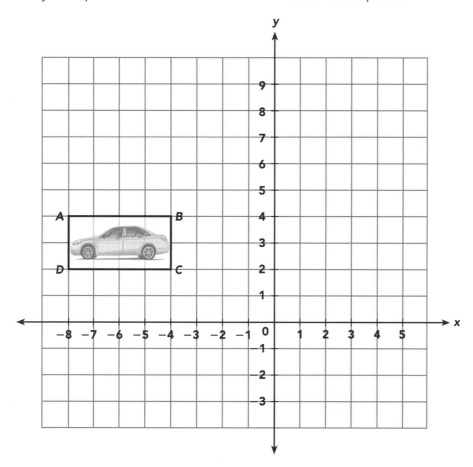

a) Johnny translated *ABCD* by 3 units to the right and 4 units up to a new position *EFGH*. Draw and label *EFGH*.

b) Tom rotated *ABCD* to a new position *IJKL* 90° clockwise about the origin, *O*. Draw and label *IJKL*.

c) Tony placed a smaller car represented as *MNOP* on the coordinate plane. *MNOP* is a dilation of *ABCD* with its center at the origin and scale factor 0.5. Draw and label *MNOP*.

6. Erika hikes through the jungle to reach her campsite. She plans to avoid the mountains since they are too dangerous to hike.

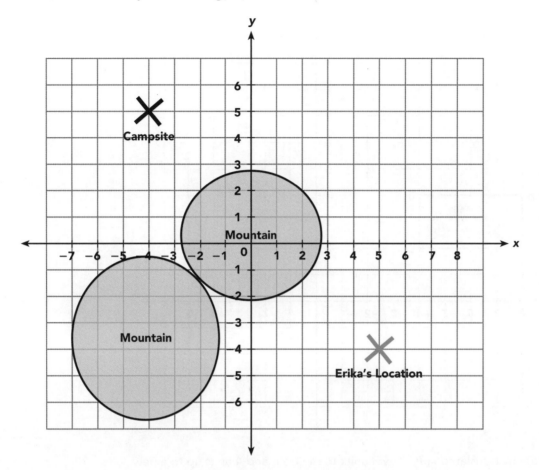

a) Draw on the coordinate grid the shortest possible path to her destination.

b) Describe the path from **a)** using a series of transformations.

7. Jenny, Kenny, Lenny, and Manny each stand at fixed positions on a parade square.

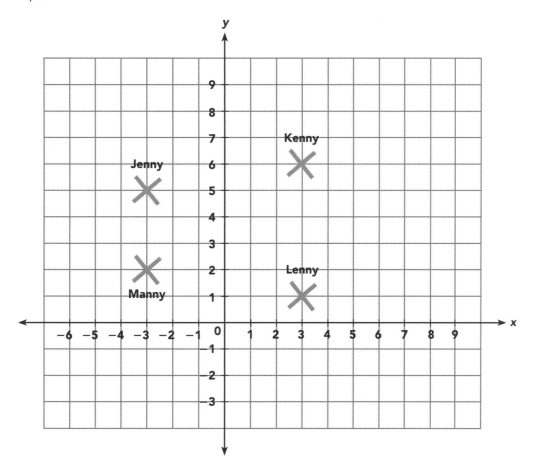

a) The parade commander calls out a command for all participants to translate 4 units down. Find the coordinates of each of the four students after the translation.

b) Find the coordinates of Jenny's and Kenny's positions after they are each reflected in the x-axis from their fixed positions.

c) Find the coordinates of each of the four students after they turn 90° counterclockwise about the origin, O from their fixed positions.

8. Timothy makes a presentation using an overhead projector, which maps his images on the computer screen onto the wall. The coordinate plane shows the relative sizes of the image *ABC* on the screen and the image *DEF* on the wall.

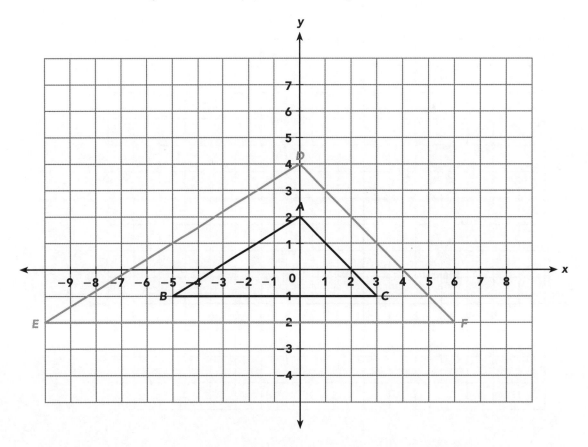

a)   Mark and label the center of dilation as *P*. Then, find the scale factor of the dilation.

b) A triangle with coordinates J (2, 3), K (−2, 0), and L (3, −1) is mapped from the computer screen onto the wall using the same center of dilation and scale factor as in **a)**. Find the coordinates of the triangle on the wall.

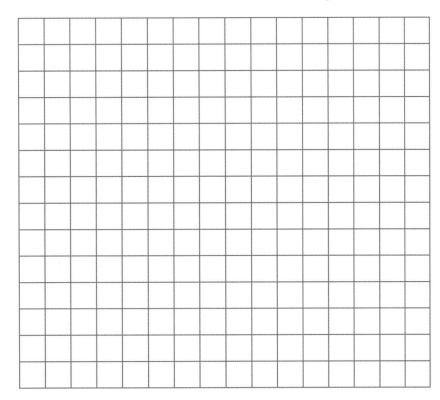

9. Johan has two tools of similar shape. He places the tools on the coordinate plane.

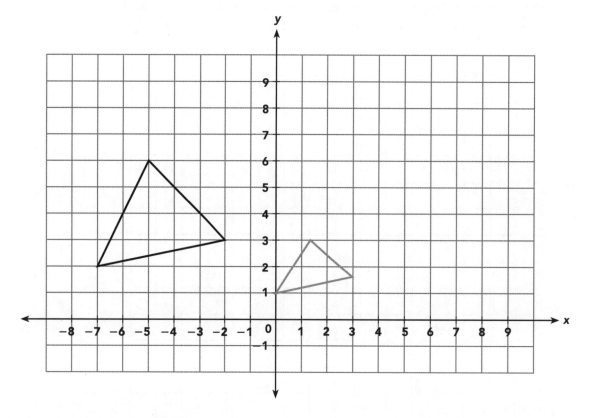

a) Label the center of dilation as *P*.

b) Describe the transformation that maps the larger tool onto the smaller tool.

10. A designer displays some pentagons on a coordinate plane. Pentagon *A* is mapped onto pentagons *B* and *C*. Pentagons *A* and *B* are shown on the coordinate plane.

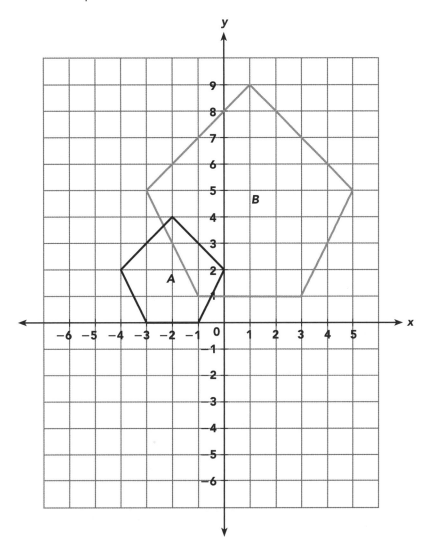

a) Describe the transformation that maps pentagon *A* onto pentagon *B*.

b) Pentagon *A* is mapped onto pentagon *C* by a reflection about the line *y* = −1. Draw pentagon *C*.

c) The transformation that maps pentagon *A* onto pentagon *C* can be described in two other ways. Describe these transformations.

d) Compare the transformations in **a)**, **b)**, and **c)** in terms of preservation of the shape and size of pentagon *A*.

11. **Brain @ Work**

Graphs of functions can be manipulated using transformations. The graph of $y = x^2 - 7$ is shown.

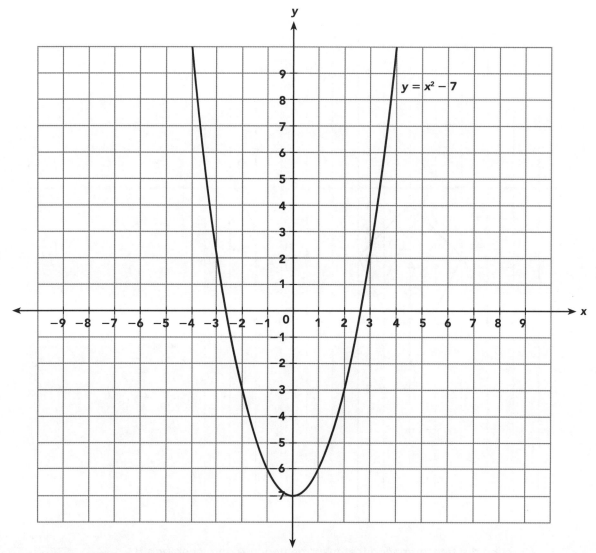

$y = x^2 - 7$

Sketch the image of the graph and state its equation after each of the following transformations.

a)   Translation of 3 units to the right

b)   Reflection in the x-axis

12. Brain @ Work

The figure below shows part of the subway map of Boston. The white circles represent stations and the grey circles represent interchanges with other subway lines. Alewife, Lechmere, Bowdoin, Oak Grove, Wonderland, and Heath are the terminal stations.

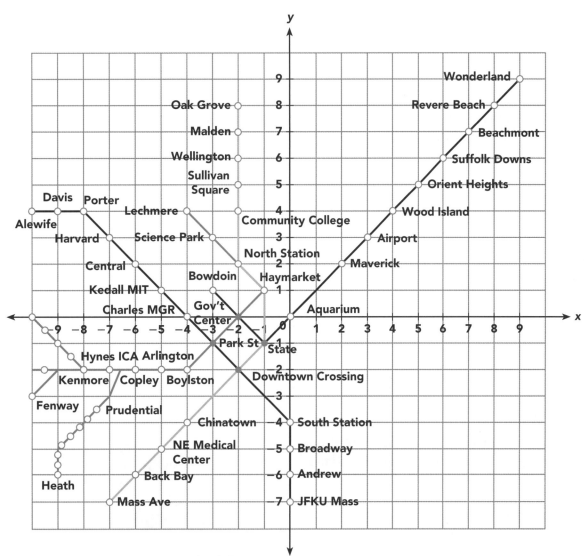

Follow the train lines to answer the following questions.

a) If Jenne were to start from the Airport, describe the train route that will take her to Porter.

b) Using the time taken to change trains to judge distance, which trip is likely to take the longest time, from Wellington to Boylston or from Wellington to Aquarium?

CHAPTER

9 Congruency and Similarity

Solve. Show your work.

1. Georgina drew a house using different shapes as shown. The area of *EFGH* is
   10.8 square centimeters and the area of *JKLM* is 2.7 square centimeters. Given
   that *EFGH* is similar to *JKLM* and *GF* is three times *CE*, find the value of *x*.

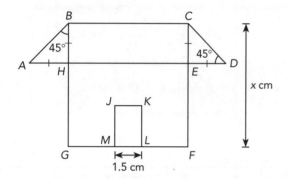

2. In the diagram, △*DEF* is an isosceles triangle
   and △*HYD* is congruent to △*XGE*. Find the
   length of each segment.

   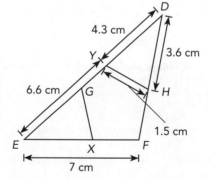

   a) $\overline{XG}$

   b) $\overline{GY}$

   c) $\overline{XF}$

3. △ABC has an area of 16 square inches and
△EBD has an area of 36 square inches.
$\overline{AC}$ is parallel to $\overline{ED}$.

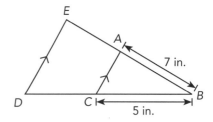

a)   State whether △ABC is similar to △EBD.
Justify your reasoning.

b)   Find the length of $\overline{EB}$.

c)   Find the length of $\overline{CD}$.

4. Toby uses similar triangles of different sizes to build a model airplane. Using
the information given in the figures, find the values of x, y, and z.

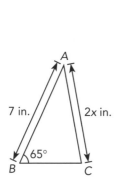

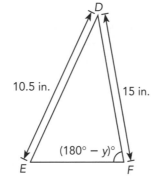

5. △*ABC* is similar to △*DEF*. Given that *AB* = 3 in., *BF* = 4 in., *DF* = 12 in., *CE* = 7 in., and *DE* = 4.5 in., find the unknown lengths.

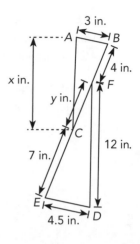

6. A large cone has a volume of 50π cubic inches. The bottom of the cone is cut off to make a smaller cone.

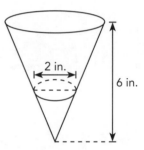

a)   What is the radius of the larger cone?

b)   What is the height of the smaller cone?

c)   What is the greatest volume of water that the smaller cone can hold in terms of π?

d)   Is the ratio of the volumes of the two cones the same as the ratio of the heights of the two cones? If not, how are they related?

7. △*ABC* is mapped onto triangle △*A′B′C′* which is then mapped onto △*A″B″C″*.
  △*ABC* and △*A″B″C″* are shown in the diagram.

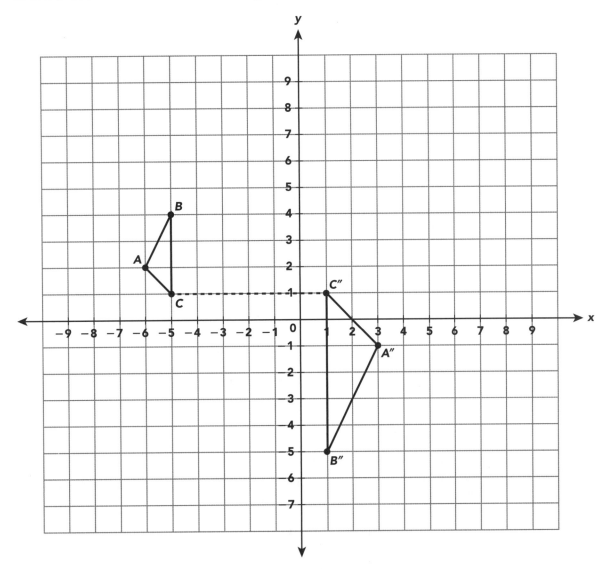

a) Describe the sequence of transformations from △*ABC* to △*A″B″C″*.

b) Describe a single transformation from △*ABC* to △*A″B″C″*.

8. Describe the sequence of transformations to move the ship from *A* to *B*.

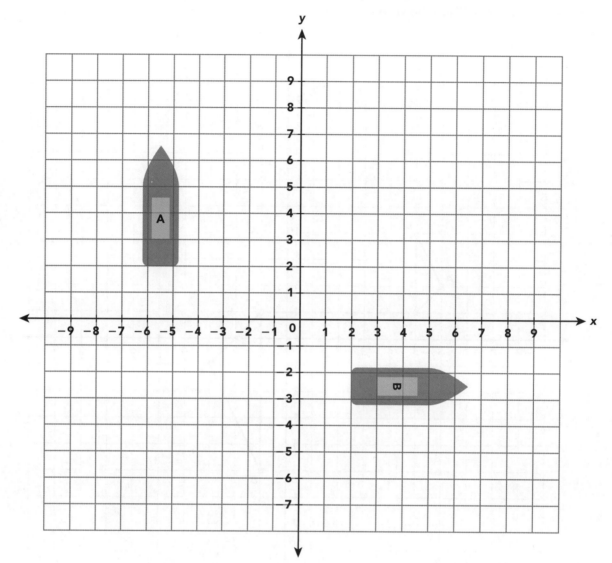

9. The actual length of a swimming pool is 50 meters. The actual area of the pool is 1,250 square meters. On a scale drawing, the area of the pool is 50 square centimeters. What is the diagonal length of the swimming pool to the nearest centimeter, on the scale drawing?

10. Anthony makes a sculpture. It has a side view *ABCDE* as shown. He places
the sculpture in front of a mirror such that it is reflected as *STUVW*.

a)   State the angles that correspond to ∠*ACB* and ∠*DCE*.

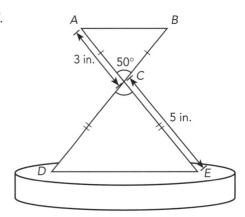

b)   Find the lengths of $\overline{TU}$ and $\overline{UV}$.

c)   Show that △*ABC* and △*EDC* are similar.

11. Brain @ Work

Elvin has three sails of different sizes for his model ships. Which of the sails
are congruent and which are similar?

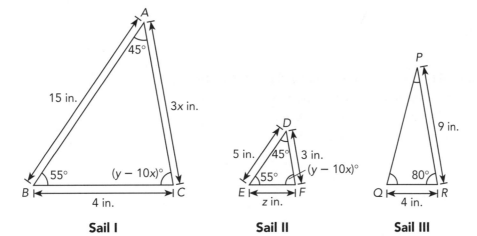

Sail I   Sail II   Sail III

12. Brain @ Work

Using photo editing software, photographs can be enlarged or reduced proportionately to different sizes. This ensures that both the original and edited photographs are similar.

a) Yasmin has a photograph measuring 5-inch by 3-inch. She wants to enlarge it to fit into a frame that measures 8-inch by 10-inch. Can this be done without cropping the photograph? Explain.

b) Jessica decides to enlarge a 3-inch by 3-inch photograph to fit a 10-inch by 10-inch frame. Will the photograph need to be cropped? If she uses Yasmin's 8-inch by 10-inch frame, will the photograph fit? Explain your answers.

c) Nicholas wants to buy a photo frame that will fit a 5-inch by 8-inch photograph once it has been enlarged. Suggest two possible sizes of photo frames he can buy such that his photo can be enlarged without being cropped. Explain your reasoning.

CHAPTER

 Statistics

1. Scientists predict that there is a relationship between the altitude of a location and the atmospheric temperature. In an experiment to determine the truth of their hypothesis, the following sets of data are collected.

Altitude (km)	0	1	2	3	4	5	6
Temperature (°C)	12.0	6.0	4.0	−3.0	−8.5	−17.0	−25.0

Altitude (km)	7	8	9	10	11	12
Temperature (°C)	−34.0	−42.0	−45.0	−49.0	−50.0	−68.0

a) Use the graph paper on the next page. Construct the scatter plot. Use 1 centimeter on the horizontal axis to represent 1 kilometer. Use 1 centimeter on the vertical axis to represent 10°C from the interval of –60°C to 20°C.

b) Identify any outlier(s).

c) Describe the association between the altitude and the temperature.

d) Draw a line of best fit and write its equation.

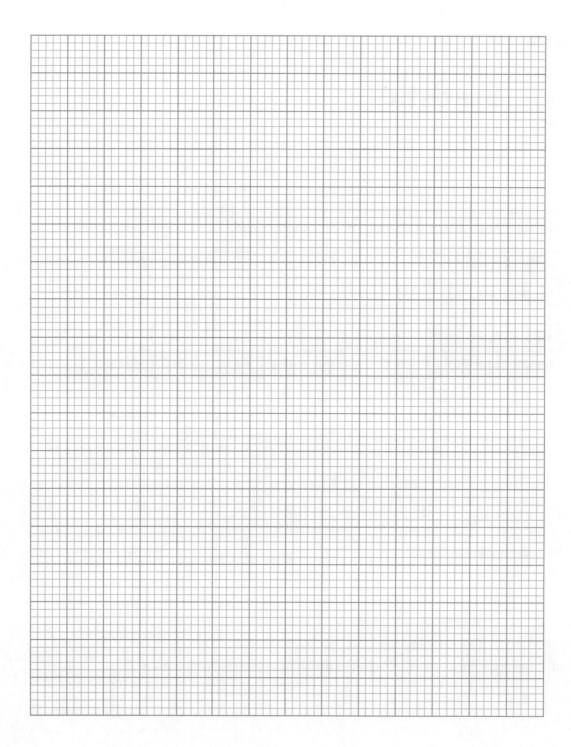

Name: _____   Date: _____

2. Marley is exploring the association between different amounts of fertilizer used and the height of plants. All his plants were planted on the same day, and watered with the same amount of water mixed with different quantities of fertilizer. He recorded the heights of the plants after a month. The scatter plot below displays bivariate data on the amount of fertilizer used, x units per milliliter, and the height of the plants, y inches.

Heights and Fertilizer Amounts of Plants

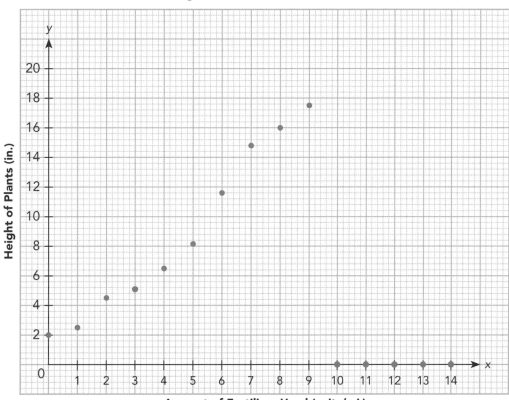

Amount of Fertilizer Used (units/mL)

a) Using data from the scatter plot, complete the data table.

Amount of Fertilizer (units per mL)	0	1	2	3	4	5	6	
Height at the End of the Month (in.)	2	2.5		5.1		8.2	11.6	14.8

Amount of Fertilizer (units per mL)	8	9	10	11	12	13	14
Height at the End of the Month (in.)		17.5	0	0	0		

b) Suggest what happened to the plants when more than 9 units per milliliter of fertilizer were added to the water.

c) Using the scatter plot, draw a line of best fit for the interval 0 to 9 units of fertilizer per millimeter. Describe the association between the amount of fertilizer and the height of the plants in this interval.

d) Based on the line of best fit, what is the minimum amount of fertilizer required for a plant to be at least 13 inches tall?

Name: _____ Date: _____

3. The size of a pumpkin can be measured in terms of its diameter, as well as its total weight. Fifteen different pumpkins were measured to determine if there is an association between the diameter of a pumpkin and its total weight.

Diameter of Pumpkin (in.)	15	23	25	24	11	17	21	34	29	20	16	28
Total Weight (lb)	6	8	13	9.5	5.4	6	8.5	17	15	7.6	6	14

a) Use the graph paper on the next page. Construct a scatter plot for this data. Use 1 centimeter on the vertical axis to represent 2 pounds. Use 1 centimeter on the horizontal axis to represent 5 inches from 15 to 30.

b) Predict the weight of a pumpkin with a diameter of 24 inches. Explain your reasoning.

c) Is your answer in **b)** the same as that of the data point where the pumpkin weighs 9.5 pounds and measures 24 inches in diameter? Explain.

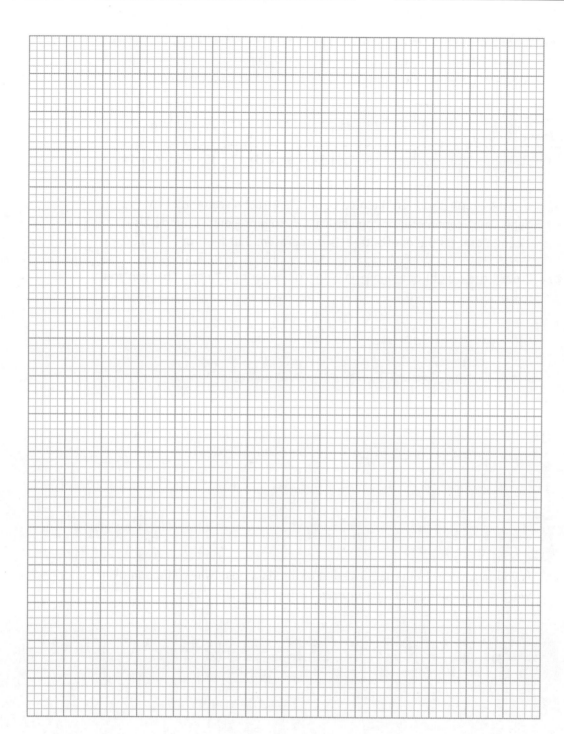

4. While it is often stated that the boiling point of water is 100°C (212°F), in reality water boils at different temperatures at different altitudes. Gerald collected data on the boiling point of water at different altitudes. His findings are as follows:

Height (ft in 1,000s)	0	2.5	6.33	1.7	9.0	1.65
Boiling Point of Water (°F)	212	207	200	209	196	209

Height (ft in 1,000s)	3.0	5.5	7.52	4.57	5.73	0.87
Boiling Point of Water (°F)	206	202	198	204	202	210

a) Use the graph paper on the next page. Construct a scatter plot for this data. Use 1 centimeter on the horizontal axis to represent 1,000 feet. Use 1 centimeter on the vertical axis to represent 2°F from the interval of 180°F to 220°F.

b) Sketch a line that appears to best fit the data and write its equation.

c) Label an additional point on the graph for the value of 3,200 feet. What is the corresponding temperature?

d) Find the altitude if the boiling point of water is 190°F.

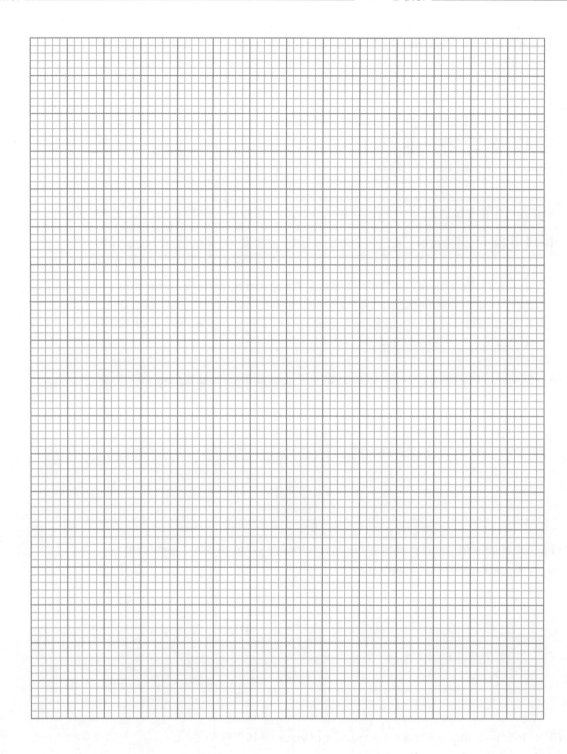

5. A tour agent offers three types of tour packages; Economic, Standard, and Deluxe to two cities, Tokyo and Hong Kong. Of the 150 customers who signed up for the package to Tokyo, 60% opted for the Economic package, 12% opted for Deluxe, and the rest opted for Standard. Of the 200 customers who signed up for the package to Hong Kong, 36 of them opted for the Deluxe package, $\frac{1}{4}$ of the remaining opted for Economic, and the rest opted for Standard.

a) Construct a two-way table to display the information.

b) What is the total number of customers who opted for the Standard tour package?

c) Describe any association between the cities visited and the type of tour packages.

6. A shop sells a certain brand of T-shirt for $23 each, a pair of pants for $48.50, and a pair of shorts for $8.40. The quantities of T-shirts, pants, and shorts sold on Monday and Tuesday are summarized in the two-way table.

Clothing Items Sold

		T-shirts	Pants	Shorts	Total
Day	**Monday**	12	5	18	
	Tuesday	8	9	20	
	Total				

a) Complete the table with the total number of each item sold on Monday and Tuesday.

b) On Monday, the store made a profit of $152.70 from selling T-shirts, pants, and shorts. The amount the store paid (the wholesale cost) for each T-shirt was $18. The wholesale cost for each pair of pants was $35. What was the wholesale cost of each pair of shorts?

c) Complete the table with the total sales of items sold on Monday.

Total Sales on Monday

		Wholesale Cost	Selling Price	Total Profit
Clothing Items	**T-Shirt**	$18 · 12 = $216	$23 · 12 = $276	$276 − $216 = $60
	Pants			
	Shorts			
	Total			$152.70

7. A bookstore carried stock of fiction titles, nonfiction titles, and reference materials for adults and children. The number of titles and reference materials at the beginning of the week is represented by the two-way table shown below:

Stock at the Beginning of the Week

Category	Fiction	Nonfiction	Reference Materials
Adult	480	235	60
Children	300	270	37

By the end of the week, the stock that remained in the bookstore is represented by another two-way table shown below:

Stock at the End of the Week

Category	Fiction	Nonfiction	Reference Materials
Adult	328	190	42
Children	140	230	10

a) Construct a third two-way table to show the number of titles and reference materials sold.

b) How many children's titles and reference materials were sold by the end of the week?

c) What was the total number of adult and children fiction titles that were sold?

d) What fraction of adult titles sold are nonfiction?

8. A restaurant gets its daily supply of seafood and vegetables from Suppliers A
and B. All the supplies are weighed in pounds. The daily supply from Monday
to Thursday, and the daily supply from Friday to Sunday are represented by the
two-way tables shown below.

Daily Supply for Monday to Thursday

Supplier		Seafood (lb)	Vegetables (lb)	Total
	A	31	16	
	B	20	22	
	Total			

Daily Supply for Friday to Sunday

Supplier		Seafood (lb)	Vegetables (lb)	Total
	A	51	35	
	B	30	25	
	Total			

a) Who supplied the greatest amount of food to the restaurant? Show how
you determined your answer.

b) What is the weekly supply of vegetables to the restaurant from both
suppliers?

c) What fraction of the weekly supply of seafood came from Supplier B?

d) Find the percent increase of the supply of seafood from both suppliers
during the weekend as compared to the weekdays. Round your answer to
the nearest tenth.

Note: Weekend includes Friday to Sunday.

Name: _____   Date: _____

9. Of the 400 students taking a second language, 70% are girls. Among the girls, $\frac{1}{5}$ of them take German, 100 girls take Spanish, and the rest take French. Among the boys, $\frac{1}{4}$ of them take French, 36 take Spanish and the rest take German.

a) Complete the two-way table below to display the data.

Language

		German	Spanish	French	Total
Gender	**Female**				
	Male				
	Total				

b) Find the relative frequencies among the rows, and interpret the meaning. Round your answers to the nearest hundredth, where necessary.

c) Find the relative frequencies among the columns, and interpret the meaning. Round your answers to the nearest hundredth, where necessary.

© Marshall Cavendish International (Singapore) Private Limited.

10. The school nurse keeps track of the number of injuries caused by playing different school-sponsored sports over the course of 3 years. Her findings are displayed in the graph.

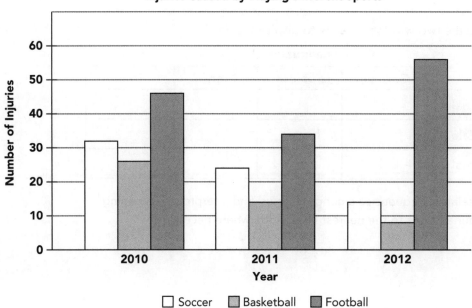

a) Use the data to construct a two-way table detailing the number of injuries sustained playing different sports.

b) By calculating the frequencies among rows and/or columns, determine which sport has the highest number of injuries and the year that has the highest frequency of injuries occurring.

11. Brain @ Work

A nutrition specialist compiles heights and mass data of some of her clients. The data are shown in the tables.

Name	Alice	Sam	Kelvin	Patricia	Owen	Bernice	Eunice	Ben	Mike	Andrew
Mass (kg)	50	70	70	65	67	46	48	56	60	70
Height (m)	1.56	2	1.78	1.63	1.89	1.5	1.53	1.8	1.65	1.77

Name	Ian	Janice	June	Peter	Susan	Tom	Royston	Amy	Nancy	Hillary
Mass (kg)	58	48	53	80	55	63	72	54	60	58
Height (m)	1.8	1.67	1.58	1.68	1.56	1.7	1.62	1.57	1.56	1.56

a) Use the graph paper on the next page. Construct the scatter plot for the data and describe the association between height and mass.

b) The Body Mass Index (BMI) is used as an indicator of a person's ideal mass and is calculated by dividing a person's mass by the product of their height, in meters $\left(\dfrac{\text{weight}}{\text{height} \cdot \text{height}} \right)$. The ideal range for a healthy BMI is between 18.5 and 25. Construct a two-way table for the data, using the categories: Male, Female, within healthy BMI range, and not within healthy BMI range. Round BMI to the nearest tenth, where necessary.

c) Find the relative frequencies to compare the distribution of genders for healthy and unhealthy BMI.

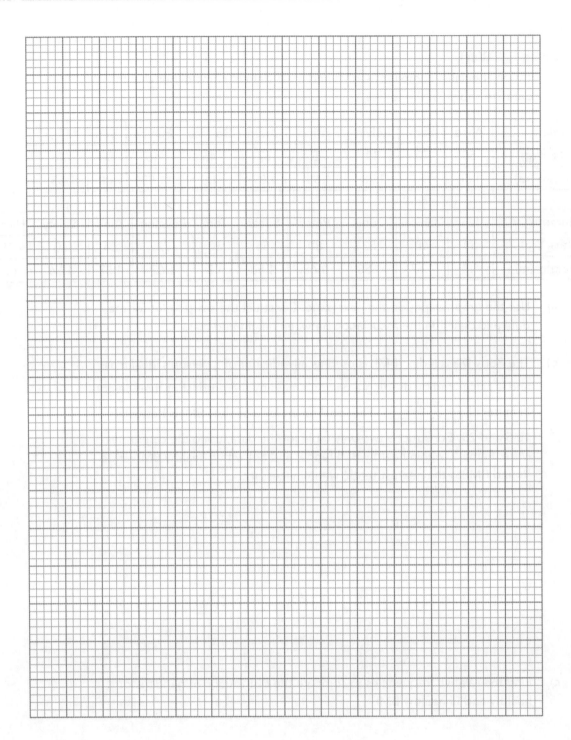

12. **Brain @ Work**

At a bank, Raj wants to change his US dollars to Euros. Before doing so, he studies the following exchange rate table.

Amount (USD) Exchanged	Exchange Rate (Euro) for 1 USD
$1 – $99	0.75
$100 – $499	0.76
$500 – $999	0.77
$1,000 – $4,999	0.78
$5,000 – $10,000	0.80

a) Complete the table showing the amounts Raj exchanges or receives in various transactions.

USD	1,000	2,500	3,600		4,200		6,200	8,000
Euros	780	1,950		3,120	3,276	4,000		6,400

b) Use the graph paper on the next page. Construct a scatter plot to show the association between the amount of money in USD and the amount of money in Euros.

c) Is the relationship between the Euros and USD exchange rate linear? Explain your answer.

Name: _____   Date: _____

Probability

Solve. Show your work.

1. Alyce spins the two pentagonal spinners shown.

 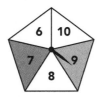

a)   Create a table to show the possible outcomes for the sum of the two spins.

b)   Find the probability of Alyce spinning the spinners and getting a sum of 10 or 12.

c)   Find the probability of Alyce spinning the spinners and getting a prime number as the sum.

2. Dave will either go swimming, or exercise in the gymnasium in the morning. If the sky is sunny, there is an 80% chance that he will go swimming. If the sky is overcast, there is a 60% chance that he will exercise in the gymnasium. If it rains, he will definitely exercise in the gymnasium. The probability of having a sunny day in the morning is 0.5. The probability of having rain in the morning is 0.2.

   a) Draw a probability tree diagram to represent the possible outcomes.

   b) What is the probability that Dave will go swimming and the sky is overcast?

   c) What is the probability that he will exercise in the gymnasium regardless of the weather condition?

3. Elaine places 20 egg sandwiches, 30 tuna sandwiches, and 20 ham sandwiches on a tray. Sam picks 2 sandwiches randomly from the tray.

   a) What is the probability that Sam picks an egg sandwich followed by a tuna sandwich?

   b) If Sam takes two ham sandwiches, what is the probability that Eliza selects two ham sandwiches?

4. A circus troupe consists of 1 ringmaster, 2 clowns, 5 trapeze artists, and 16 acrobats.

   a) For an interview, a news reporter picks one member of the troupe. What is the probability that the reporter interviews a trapeze artist?

   b) Three members of the troupe are selected to appear on a publicity poster. What is the probability that out of the 3 selected members, 2 are acrobats?

   c) What is the probability that the ringmaster is not selected to appear on the publicity poster in b)?

5. Trudi can either walk to school, or she can take the bus. The probability of her taking the bus on any given day is 0.77.

    a) Assuming that her choice of transport on any given day is independent of her choice of transport on another day, find out the probability of her taking the bus to school on exactly 3 days, out of a total of 5 days.

    b) Find the probability that the 3 days in **a)** happen consecutively.

6. Sapphira can borrow two reading materials from the library. The bar chart below shows the types of reading materials available in the school library.

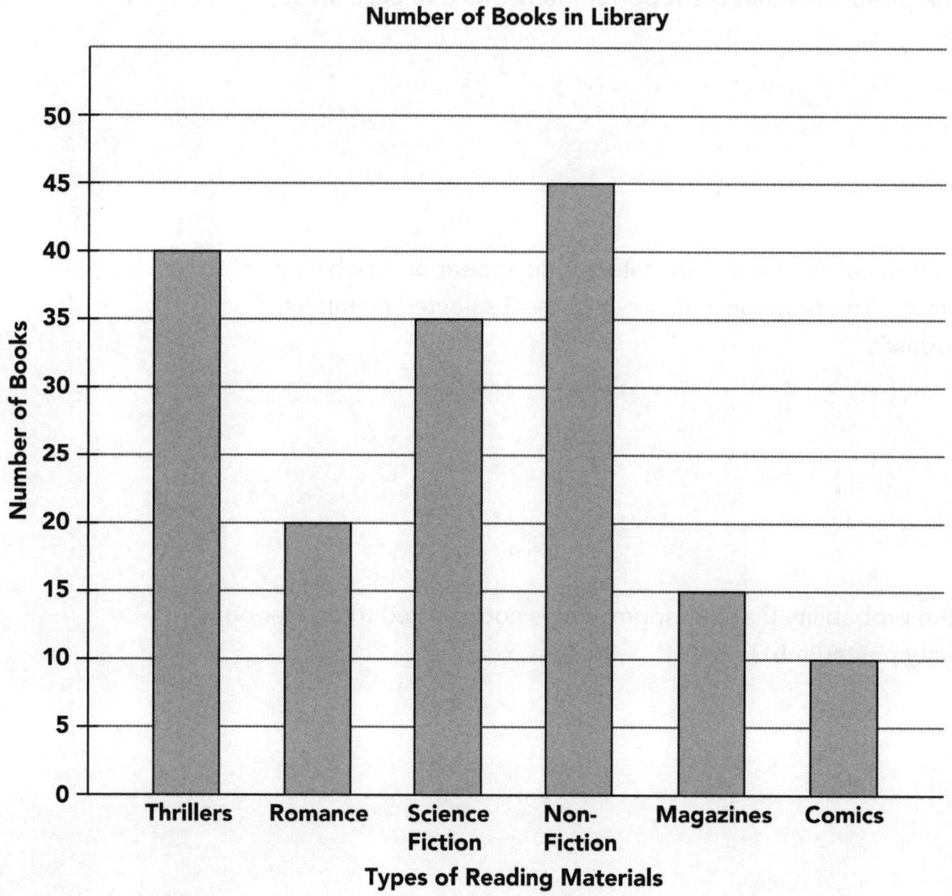

Number of Books in Library

a) Using the bar chart, find the probability that the two reading materials Sapphira borrows are fiction (romance, thriller and science-fiction) books.

b) Is it more likely that Sapphira borrows both a magazine and a comic, or a romance and thriller? Explain your reasoning.

7. June works part-time 7 days a week. She meets a friend for dinner after work twice a week.

   a)   Assuming that she met her friend on Monday, what is the probability that she meets her friend again on Tuesday?

   b)   If she does not meet her friend on Monday or Tuesday, what is the probability that she meets her friend on Wednesday?

8. Mary has 10 red, 4 green, 2 blue, 4 orange, 3 purple, 2 peach, and 2 pink dresses in her closet. She wears one dress at random every day, and no two dresses are the same.

   a)   What are the chances of Mary choosing the same dress 2 days in a row?

   b)   Assuming that Mary chooses to bring 5 dresses on a vacation, what are the chances that she does not bring an orange dress?

© Marshall Cavendish International (Singapore) Private Limited.

9. A mall holds a 'Spin and Win' event. Players spin a wheel in an attempt to win the prize written on the panels of the wheel. Before each turn, players have to throw a 6-sided die. The player that obtains the largest value on a throw is then allowed to spin the wheel. James, Charles, and Stacey take part in the game.

a) Given that James throws a "5", what is the probability that he gets to spin the wheel?

b) In addition to the panels detailing the prizes to be won, 3 out of 25 panels are "black hole" panels where players do not get to win any prize. If Charles and Stacey throw a "3" and "4", what is the possibility of James not winning a prize?

10. The probability diagram represents the likelihood of Santhi being late for school if she wakes up late.

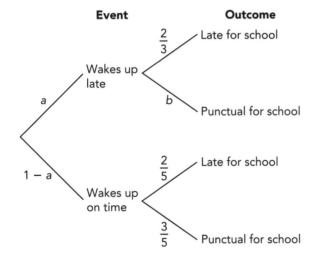

Event

Outcome

$\frac{2}{3}$ — Late for school

Wakes up late

a

b

Punctual for school

$1 - a$

Wakes up on time

$\frac{2}{5}$ — Late for school

$\frac{3}{5}$ — Punctual for school

a) Given that Santhi does not wake up late $\frac{8}{25}$ of the time, find the unknowns a and b.

b) Is Santhi more likely to be punctual or late on any given day? Explain your answer.

11. Brain @ Work

Joanna, Marsha, and Alena are playing a game where they toss a fair coin and spin a fair spinner as shown on the right. Three points are given when the coin lands on heads and one point is given when the coin lands on tails. Each number on the spinner represents the number of points awarded. If the toss lands on heads, the player gets to spin the spinner once. If the toss lands on tails, the player gets to spin the spinner twice. A player wins when the sum of her points is greater than 8.

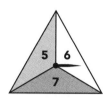

a) Draw a probability tree diagram to represent the possible outcomes.

b) What is the probability of winning the game if the first toss lands on heads?

c) What is the probability of getting a sum of 9 or 12 points?

Name: _____   Date: _____

12. **Brain @ Work**

Violet can take different routes to get from her office to her house. The probability of her taking a particular route depends on whether the road is congested. Her travel time depends on the distance traveled.

a) Complete the probability table shown.

Route	Probability of Being Congested	Probability of Not Being Congested
Office – Sixth Avenue	0.2	0.8
Sixth Avenue – East Park	0.55	
East Park – Home	0.6	0.4
Office – City Center		0.3
City Center – Home		0.8
Office – North Bridge Highway	0.6	
North Bridge Highway – Home	0.45	0.55

b) Given the route diagram, which route is she most likely to take? Justify your reasoning.

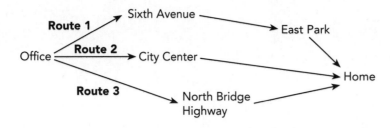

Answers

Chapter 1

1. a) $\dfrac{(5^2)^4 \cdot 3^{10} \cdot 5^2}{15^2 \cdot 3^0}$

$= \dfrac{5^{2 \cdot 4} \cdot 3^{10} \cdot 5^2}{15^2 \cdot 3^0}$

$= \dfrac{5^8 \cdot 3^{10} \cdot 5^2}{15^2 \cdot 3^0}$

$= \dfrac{5^{8+2} \cdot 3^{10}}{15^2 \cdot 3^0}$

$= \dfrac{5^{10} \cdot 3^{10}}{15^2 \cdot 1}$

$= \dfrac{(5 \cdot 3)^{10}}{15^2 \cdot 1}$

$= \dfrac{15^{10}}{15^2}$

$= 15^{10-2}$

$= 15^8$

b) $\dfrac{(7^5 \cdot 7^3)^4 \cdot 7^{-2}}{7^{-7} \cdot 7^{20}}$

$= \dfrac{(7^{5+3})^4 \cdot 7^{-2}}{7^{-7+20}}$

$= \dfrac{(7^8)^4 \cdot 7^{-2}}{7^{13}}$

$= \dfrac{7^{8 \cdot 4} \cdot 7^{-2}}{7^{13}}$

$= \dfrac{7^{32} \cdot 7^{-2}}{7^{13}}$

$= \dfrac{7^{32-2}}{7^{13}}$

$= \dfrac{7^{30}}{7^{13}}$

$= 7^{30-13}$

$= 7^{17}$

c) $\dfrac{(-0.2)^4 \cdot (0.5)^4}{(0.5)^{-5} \cdot (-0.2)^{-5}}$

$= \dfrac{[(-0.2) \cdot 0.5]^4}{[0.5 \cdot (-0.2)]^{-5}}$

$= \dfrac{(-0.1)^4}{(-0.1)^{-5}}$

$= (-0.1)^{4-(-5)}$

$= (-0.1)^{4+5}$

$= (-0.1)^9$

$= -0.1^9$

d) $\left(-\dfrac{6}{35}\right)^3 \cdot \left(-\dfrac{7}{15}\right)^3 \cdot \left(\dfrac{10}{21}\right)^3$

$= \left[\left(-\dfrac{6}{35}\right) \cdot \left(-\dfrac{7}{15}\right) \cdot \dfrac{10}{21}\right]^3$

$= \left(\dfrac{4}{105}\right)^3$

2. a) $\left(\dfrac{4}{6}a^2b^2\right)^3$

$= \left(\dfrac{2}{3}a^2b^2\right)^3$

$= \left(\dfrac{2}{3}\right)^3 \cdot (a^2)^3 \cdot (b^2)^3$

$= \left(\dfrac{2}{3}\right)^3 \cdot a^{2 \cdot 3} \cdot b^{2 \cdot 3}$

$= \dfrac{8}{27}a^6b^6$

b) $4b^2(3a^2b^5)^{-2}$

$= \dfrac{4b^2}{(3a^2b^5)^2}$

$= \dfrac{4b^2}{3^2 \cdot (a^2)^2 \cdot (b^5)^2}$

$= \dfrac{4b^2}{3^2 \cdot a^{2 \cdot 2} \cdot b^{5 \cdot 2}}$

$= \dfrac{4b^2}{9a^4b^{10}}$

$= \dfrac{4}{9} \cdot a^{-4} \cdot b^2 \cdot b^{-10}$

$= \dfrac{4}{9} \cdot a^{-4} \cdot b^{2-10}$

$= \dfrac{4}{9} \cdot a^{-4} \cdot b^{-8}$

$= \dfrac{4}{9a^4b^8}$

c) $\dfrac{81g^{-2} \cdot \left(\dfrac{1}{3}k\right)^{-3}}{27g^{-4}k^{-5}}$

$= \dfrac{81g^{-2} \cdot \left(\dfrac{1}{3}\right)^{-3} \cdot k^{-3}}{27g^{-4}k^{-5}}$

$= \dfrac{81}{27 \cdot \left(\dfrac{1}{3}\right)^3} \cdot g^{-2} \cdot g^4 \cdot k^{-3} \cdot k^5$

$= \dfrac{81}{27 \cdot \dfrac{1}{27}} \cdot g^{-2+4} \cdot k^{-3+5}$

$= 81g^2k^2$

d) $\dfrac{\sqrt{64a^4} \cdot b^4}{64ab^2}$

$= \dfrac{8a^2 \cdot b^4}{64ab^2}$

$= \dfrac{8a^2 \cdot b^4}{8^2 \cdot a \cdot b^2}$

$= 8 \cdot 8^{-2} \cdot a^2 \cdot a^{-1} \cdot b^4 \cdot b^{-2}$

$= 8^{1-2} \cdot a^{2-1} \cdot b^{4-2}$

$= 8^{-1} \cdot a \cdot b^2$

$= \dfrac{ab^2}{8}$

3. Volume of a small cube $= 1.2 \cdot 1.2 \cdot 1.2$

$\qquad\qquad\qquad\qquad = 1.728 \text{ in}^2$

Volume of cuboid $= 58.8$

$\qquad 1.728x = 58.8$

$\qquad\qquad x \approx 34$

4. a) Population of amoeba colony after 4 divisions

$= 160 \cdot 2^4$

$= 2{,}560$

b) Let n be the number of divisions.

$160 \cdot 2^n = 40{,}960$

$2^n = \dfrac{40{,}960}{160}$

$2^n = 256$

$2^n = 2^8$

$n = 8$

5. a) Thickness of paper

$= 0.38 \cdot 2^7$

$= 48.64 \text{ mm}$

b) Let n be the number of times the paper has been folded.

$0.38 \cdot 2^n = 12.16$

$2^n = \dfrac{12.16}{0.38}$

$2^n = 32$

$2^n = 2^5$

$n = 5$

6. a) First number $= 3$

Second number $= 3^2$

$\qquad\qquad\qquad = 9$

Third number $= 3^3$

$\qquad\qquad\qquad = 27$

Fourth number $= 3^4$

$\qquad\qquad\qquad = 81$

Fifth number $= 3^5$

$\qquad\qquad\qquad = 243$

Sixth number $= 3^6$

$\qquad\qquad\qquad = 729$

Seventh number $= 3^7$

$\qquad\qquad\qquad\quad = 2{,}187$

Eighth number $= 3^8$

$\qquad\qquad\qquad = 6{,}561$

Ninth number $= 3^9$

$\qquad\qquad\qquad = 19{,}683$

Tenth number $= 3^{10}$

$\qquad\qquad\qquad = 59{,}049$

b) From **a)**, the eighth number is $3^8 = 6{,}561$. So, $n = 8$.

7. Volume of cylindrical cup $= \pi r^2 \cdot 7 = 112\pi$

$\pi r^2 \cdot 7 = 112\pi$

$7\pi r^2 = 112\pi$

$r^2 = \dfrac{112\pi}{7\pi}$

$r^2 = 16$

$r = \sqrt{16}$

$r = 4 \text{ cm}$

Volume of cone $= \dfrac{1}{3}\pi r^2 h = 112\pi$

$\dfrac{1}{3}\pi(4^2)h = 112\pi$

$\dfrac{1}{3}\pi \cdot 16 \cdot h = 112\pi$

$\dfrac{16}{3}\pi h = 112\pi$

$h = \dfrac{112\pi}{\dfrac{16}{3}\pi}$

$h = 21$

The height of the cone is 21 centimeters.

8. a) Volume of cube $= s^3 = 64$

$s = \sqrt[3]{64}$

$s = 4 \text{ inches}$

b) Let the radius be r inches.

Volume of sphere $= \dfrac{4}{3}\pi r^3 = 64$

$\dfrac{3}{4} \cdot \dfrac{4}{3}\pi r^3 = 64 \cdot \dfrac{3}{4}$

$\pi r^3 = 48$

$\dfrac{\pi r^3}{\pi} = \dfrac{48}{\pi}$

$r^3 \approx 15.279$

$r = \sqrt[3]{15.279}$

$r \approx 2.48 \text{ inches}$

c) Surface area of cube $= 6 \cdot 4^2$

$\qquad\qquad\qquad\qquad\quad = 96 \text{ in}^2$

Surface area of sphere $= 4\pi r^2$

$\qquad\qquad\qquad\qquad = 4 \cdot \pi \cdot (2.48)^2$

$\qquad\qquad\qquad\qquad \approx 77.3 \text{ in}^2$

Since $96 \text{ in}^2 > 77.3 \text{ in}^2$, the cube has a greater surface area.

9. a)   1,008

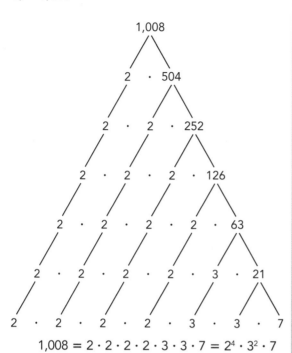

$$1{,}008 = 2 \cdot 2 \cdot 2 \cdot 2 \cdot 3 \cdot 3 \cdot 7 = 2^4 \cdot 3^2 \cdot 7$$

b)   864

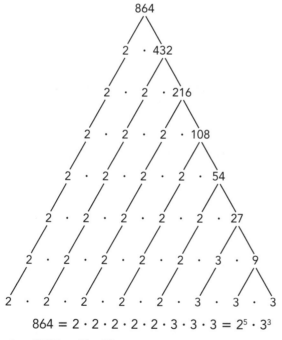

$$864 = 2 \cdot 2 \cdot 2 \cdot 2 \cdot 2 \cdot 3 \cdot 3 \cdot 3 = 2^5 \cdot 3^3$$

c)   GCF $= 2^4 \cdot 3^2$

10. Let the radius of the cell be r m.

$$r = \frac{d}{2}$$

$$r = \frac{10^{-5}}{2}$$

$$r = \frac{1}{200{,}000} \text{ m}$$

Volume of 10 trillion cells

$$= \frac{4}{3}\pi r^3 \cdot 10^{13}$$

$$= \frac{4}{3} \cdot \pi \cdot \left(\frac{1}{200{,}000}\right)^3 \cdot 10^{13}$$

$$= 5.24 \cdot 10^{-3}$$

The volume of 10 trillion cells is $5.24 \cdot 10^{-3}$ cubic meter.

11. Brain@Work

a)

(i)
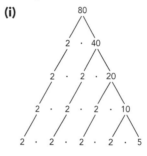

(ii)
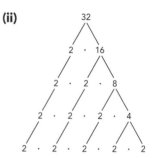

(iii)   **(iv)**
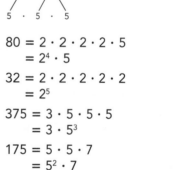

$$80 = 2 \cdot 2 \cdot 2 \cdot 2 \cdot 5$$
$$ = 2^4 \cdot 5$$
$$32 = 2 \cdot 2 \cdot 2 \cdot 2 \cdot 2$$
$$ = 2^5$$
$$375 = 3 \cdot 5 \cdot 5 \cdot 5$$
$$ = 3 \cdot 5^3$$
$$175 = 5 \cdot 5 \cdot 7$$
$$ = 5^2 \cdot 7$$

b)   LCM of 80, 32, 375, and 175
$$= 2^5 \cdot 3 \cdot 5^3 \cdot 7$$
$$= 84{,}000 \text{ minutes}$$
$$= 1{,}400 \text{ hours}$$
$$= 58\frac{1}{3} \text{ days}$$
$$= 58 \text{ days } 8 \text{ hours}$$

The next concurrent eruption of the four geysers will occur in 58 days at 5:00 P.M.

12. Brain@Work

a) Interest and principal amount at the end of year 1

$$= 2{,}500 \cdot 5\% + 2{,}500$$
$$= 2{,}500 \cdot \frac{5}{100} + 2{,}500$$
$$= 2{,}500 \cdot \frac{5}{100} + 2{,}500 \cdot \frac{100}{100}$$
$$= 2{,}500 \cdot \left(\frac{5}{100} + \frac{100}{100}\right)$$
$$= 2{,}500 \cdot \left(\frac{105}{100}\right)$$
$$= 2{,}500 \cdot 1.05$$

Interest and principal amount at the end of year 2
$$= (2{,}500 \cdot 1.05) \cdot 1.05$$
$$= 2{,}500 \cdot 1.05^2$$

Interest and principal amount at the end of 2017 (5th year)
$$= P(1 + r)^n$$
$$= 2{,}500 \cdot 1.05^5$$
$$= \$3{,}190.70$$

b) Total amount at the end of year 1
$$= 2{,}500 \cdot 1.05$$

Total amount at the end of year 2
$$= (2{,}500 \cdot 1.05 + 200) \cdot 1.05$$
$$= 2{,}500 \cdot 1.05^2 + 200 \cdot 1.05$$

Total amount at the end of the year 3
$$= (2{,}500 \cdot 1.05^2 + 200 \cdot 1.05 + 200) \cdot 1.05$$
$$= 2{,}500 \cdot 1.05^3 + 200 \cdot 1.05^2 + 200 \cdot 1.05$$

Total amount at the end of the year 4
$$= (2{,}500 \cdot 1.05^3 + 200 \cdot 1.05^2 + 200 \cdot 1.05 + 200) \cdot 1.05$$
$$= 2{,}500 \cdot 1.05^4 + 200 \cdot 1.05^3 + 200 \cdot 1.05^2 + 200 \cdot 1.05$$

Total amount at the end of the year 5
$$= (2{,}500 \cdot 1.05^4 + 200 \cdot 1.05^3 + 200 \cdot 1.05^2 + 200 \cdot 1.05 + 200) \cdot 1.05$$
$$= 2{,}500 \cdot 1.05^5 + 200 \cdot 1.05^4 + 200 \cdot 1.05^3 + 200 \cdot 1.05^2 + 200 \cdot 1.05$$
$$= \$4{,}095.83$$

c) Fixed yearly interest
$$= 2{,}500 \cdot 5\% \cdot 5 \text{ years}$$
$$= \$625$$

Total amount at the end of 2017
$$= 2{,}500 + 625$$
$$= \$3{,}125$$

Since $\$3{,}190.70 > \$3{,}125$, the compound interest account will result in a greater balance.

Chapter 2

1. a)

State	Population	
	Standard Form	Scientific Notation
Florida	19,060,000	$1.906 \cdot 10^7$
Washington	6,839,000	$6.839 \cdot 10^6$
Tennessee	6,403,000	$6.403 \cdot 10^6$
New York	19,450,000	$1.945 \cdot 10^7$
Wisconsin	5,712,000	$5.712 \cdot 10^6$
Minnesota	5,345,000	$5.345 \cdot 10^6$

b) Total population of Florida and Wisconsin
$$= 1.906 \cdot 10^7 + 5.712 \cdot 10^6$$
$$= 19.06 \cdot 10^6 + 5.712 \cdot 10^6$$
$$= (19.06 + 5.712) \cdot 10^6$$
$$= 24.722 \cdot 10^6$$
$$= 2.4722 \cdot 10^7$$

Total population of New York and Minnesota
$$= 1.945 \cdot 10^7 + 5.345 \cdot 10^6$$
$$= 19.45 \cdot 10^6 + 5.345 \cdot 10^6$$
$$= (19.45 + 5.345) \cdot 10^6$$
$$= 24.795 \cdot 10^6$$
$$= 2.4795 \cdot 10^7$$

Since the exponents are the same, compare the coefficients.
$$2.4795 > 2.4772$$
So, $2.4795 \cdot 10^7 > 2.4772 \cdot 10^7$.
New York and Minnesota have a greater total population than Florida and Wisconsin.

2. Distance from New York to Paris
$$= \text{Speed} \cdot \text{Time}$$
$$= 1{,}334 \cdot 3.5$$
$$= 4{,}669 \text{ mi}$$

Speed of a commercial aircraft
$$= \frac{4{,}669}{8}$$
$$= 583.625$$
$$= 5.84 \cdot 10^2 \text{ mi/h}$$

The speed of the commercial aircraft is about $5.84 \cdot 10^2$ miles per hour.

3. a) Speed of snail = 0.002 mi = $2 \cdot 10^{-3}$ mi

Speed of cheetah = 60 mi = $6 \cdot 10$ mi

$$\frac{\text{Speed of snail}}{\text{Speed of cheetah}} = \frac{2 \cdot 10^{-3}}{6 \cdot 10}$$

$$= \frac{2}{6} \cdot \frac{10^{-3}}{10}$$

$$= \frac{1}{3} \cdot 10^{-3-1}$$

$$= \frac{1}{3} \cdot 10^{-4}$$

$$= \frac{1}{3} \cdot \frac{1}{10,000}$$

$$= \frac{1}{30,000}$$

b) $\frac{1}{3} \cdot 10^{-4} \approx 0.3 \cdot 10^{-4}$

$= 3 \cdot 10^{-5}$

c) $\frac{1}{3} \cdot 10^{-4} \approx 0.333 \cdot 10^{-4}$

$= 0.0000333$

4. a) Length: 8,300,000 ft = $8.3 \cdot 10^6$ ft

Width: 230,000 ft = $2.3 \cdot 10^5$ ft

Depth: 36,000 ft = $3.6 \cdot 10^4$ ft

b) Approximate volume of water

$= 8.3 \cdot 10^6 \cdot 2.3 \cdot 10^5 \cdot 3.6 \cdot 10^4$

$= 8.3 \cdot 2.3 \cdot 3.6 \cdot 10^6 \cdot 10^5 \cdot 10^4$

$= 68.724 \cdot 10^{6+5+4}$

$= 68.724 \cdot 10^{15}$

$\approx 6.9 \cdot 10^{16}$ ft^3

5. 1 μm = $1 \cdot 10^{-6}$ m

0.3 μm = $0.3 \cdot 1 \cdot 10^{-6}$

$= 3 \cdot 10^{-7}$ m

1 m = 39.37 in.

$3 \cdot 10^{-7}$ m $= 3 \cdot 10^{-7} \cdot 39.37$

$= 3 \cdot 39.37 \cdot 10^{-7}$

$= 118.11 \cdot 10^{-7}$

$= 1.1811 \cdot 10^{-5}$ in.

6. Total time = 10.5 years

$= 10.5 \cdot 365 \cdot 24$

$= 91,980$ h

$= 9.198 \cdot 10^4$ h

Distance between Earth's solar system and Epsilon Eridani

= Speed · Time

$= 6.7 \cdot 10^8 \cdot 9.198 \cdot 10^4$

$= 6.7 \cdot 9.198 \cdot 10^8 \cdot 10^4$

$= 61.6266 \cdot 10^{8+4}$

$= 61.6266 \cdot 10^{12}$

$\approx 6.16 \cdot 10^{13}$ mi

7. a) Height of an average American male:

1 ft = 12 in.

5 ft $9\frac{1}{2}$ in. = $5 \cdot 12 + 9.5$ in.

$= 60 + 9.5$

$= 69.5$

$= 6.95 \cdot 10$ in.

Body length of a fairyfly:

0.0055 in. = $5.5 \cdot 10^{-3}$ in.

$$\frac{\text{Height of average male}}{\text{Length of fairyfly}}$$

$$= \frac{6.95 \cdot 10}{5.5 \cdot 10^{-3}}$$

$$= \frac{6.95}{5.5} \cdot \frac{10}{10^{-3}}$$

$\approx 1.3 \cdot 10^{1-(-3)}$

$= 1.3 \cdot 10^4$

The average height of the American male is about $1.3 \cdot 10^4$ times as large as the fairyfly.

b) Length of a blue whale:

110 ft = $110 \cdot 12$

$= 1,320$ in.

$= 1.32 \cdot 10^3$ in.

$$\frac{\text{Height of average male}}{\text{Length of blue whale}}$$

$$= \frac{6.95 \cdot 10}{1.32 \cdot 10^3}$$

$$= \frac{6.95}{1.32} \cdot \frac{10}{10^3}$$

$\approx 5.3 \cdot 10^{1-3}$

$= 5.3 \cdot 10^{-2}$

The average height of the American male is about $5.3 \cdot 10^{-2}$ times as large as a blue whale.

8. a) $0.24 = 2.4 \cdot 10^{-1}$

Number of people working in the 'Sales and office' category

$= 2.4 \cdot 10^{-1} \cdot 1.4 \cdot 10^8$

$= 2.4 \cdot 1.4 \cdot 10^{-1} \cdot 10^8$

$= 3.36 \cdot 10^{-1+8}$

$= 3.36 \cdot 10^7$

b) $0.01 = 1 \cdot 10^{-2}$

Number of people working in the 'Farming, forestry, and fishing' category

$= 1 \cdot 10^{-2} \cdot 1.4 \cdot 10^8$

$= 1 \cdot 1.4 \cdot 10^{-2} \cdot 10^8$

$= 1.4 \cdot 10^{-2+8}$

$= 1.4 \cdot 10^6$

$0.37 = 3.7 \cdot 10^{-1}$

Number of people working in the 'Managerial, professional, and technical' category

$= 3.7 \cdot 10^{-1} \cdot 1.4 \cdot 10^8$

$= 3.7 \cdot 1.4 \cdot 10^{-1} \cdot 10^8$

$= 5.18 \cdot 10^{-1+8}$

$= 5.18 \cdot 10^7$

9. a) $\quad$ 1 nm $\approx 3.9 \cdot 10^{-8}$ in.

$\qquad$ 120 nm $\approx 120 \cdot 3.9 \cdot 10^{-8}$

$\qquad\qquad\quad = 468 \cdot 10^{-8}$

$\qquad\qquad\quad = 4.68 \cdot 10^{-6}$ in.

The length of the H1N1 virus is about $4.68 \cdot 10^{-6}$ inch.

b) $\quad \dfrac{3.9 \cdot 10^{-5}}{4.68 \cdot 10^{-6}} = \dfrac{3.9}{4.68} \cdot \dfrac{10^{-5}}{10^{-6}}$

$\qquad\qquad\qquad \approx 0.833 \cdot 10^{-5 - (-6)}$

$\qquad\qquad\qquad = 0.833 \cdot 10$

$\qquad\qquad\qquad = 8.33$

The virus has to be 8.33 times as large as its actual size to be seen under a standard optical microscope.

10. a) $\quad$ Mass of an electron

$\qquad = \dfrac{1}{1,838} \cdot$ Mass of a neutron

$\qquad$ Mass of a neutron

$\qquad = 1,838 \cdot$ Mass of an electron

$\qquad = 1,838 \cdot 9.11 \cdot 10^{-31}$

$\qquad = 16,744.18 \cdot 10^{-31}$

$\qquad \approx 1.674 \cdot 10^{-27}$ kg

b) $\quad$ Mass of an electron

$\qquad = \dfrac{1}{1,836} \cdot$ Mass of a proton

$\qquad$ Mass of a neutron

$\qquad = 1,836 \cdot$ Mass of an electron

$\qquad = 1,836 \cdot 9.11 \cdot 10^{-31}$

$\qquad = 16,725.96 \cdot 10^{-31}$

$\qquad \approx 1.673 \cdot 10^{-27}$ kg

11. a) $\quad$ 93,000,000 mi $= 9.3 \cdot 10^{7}$ mi

b) $\quad$ 240,000 mi $= 2.4 \cdot 10^{5}$ mi

Let the distance between the moon and the Earth in Daniel's model be x.

Using a proportion:

$\qquad \dfrac{3}{9.3 \cdot 10^{7}} = \dfrac{x}{2.4 \cdot 10^{5}}$

$\qquad x \cdot 9.3 \cdot 10^{7} = 3 \cdot 2.4 \cdot 10^{5}$

$\qquad\qquad\quad x = \dfrac{7.2 \cdot 10^{5}}{9.3 \cdot 10^{7}}$

$\qquad\qquad\qquad = \dfrac{7.2}{9.3} \cdot \dfrac{10^{5}}{10^{7}}$

$\qquad\qquad\qquad \approx 0.77 \cdot 10^{5-7}$

$\qquad\qquad\qquad = 0.77 \cdot 10^{-2}$

$\qquad\qquad\qquad = 7.7 \cdot 10^{-3}$

The distance in Daniel's model would be $7.7 \cdot 10^{-3}$ foot.

c) $\quad$ Let the least actual distance from the Earth to Jupiter be x.

Using a proportion:

$\qquad \dfrac{3}{9.3 \cdot 10^{7}} = \dfrac{12.6}{x}$

$\qquad 3x = 12.6 \cdot 9.3 \cdot 10^{7}$

$\qquad \dfrac{3x}{3} = \dfrac{12.6 \cdot 9.3 \cdot 10^{7}}{3}$

$\qquad\quad x = 39.06 \cdot 10^{7}$

$\qquad\qquad = 3.906 \cdot 10^{8}$

The least actual distance from the Earth to Jupiter is $3.906 \cdot 10^{8}$ miles.

Let the greatest actual distance from the Earth to Jupiter be y.

Using a proportion:

$\qquad \dfrac{3}{9.3 \cdot 10^{7}} = \dfrac{18.6}{y}$

$\qquad 3y = 18.6 \cdot 9.3 \cdot 10^{7}$

$\qquad \dfrac{3y}{3} = \dfrac{18.6 \cdot 9.3 \cdot 10^{7}}{3}$

$\qquad\quad y = 57.66 \cdot 10^{7}$

$\qquad\qquad = 5.766 \cdot 10^{8}$

The greatest actual distance from the Earth to Jupiter is $5.766 \cdot 10^{8}$ miles.

The actual range is $3.906 \cdot 10^{8}$ miles to $5.766 \cdot 10^{8}$ miles.

12. a) $\quad$ Number of Internet users in 2006

$\qquad = 1,093 \cdot 10^{6}$

$\qquad = 1.093 \cdot 10^{9}$

$\qquad$ Number of Internet users in 2007

$\qquad = 1,262,000,000$

$\qquad = 1.262 \cdot 10^{9}$

$\qquad$ Difference between the number of Internet users in 2006 and 2007

$\qquad = 1.262 \cdot 10^{9} - 1.093 \cdot 10^{9}$

$\qquad = (1.262 - 1.093) \cdot 10^{9}$

$\qquad = 0.169 \cdot 10^{9}$

$\qquad = 1.69 \cdot 10^{8}$

b) $\quad$ Number of Internet users in 2008

$\qquad = 1,400 \cdot 10^{6}$

$\qquad = 1.4 \cdot 10^{9}$

$\qquad$ Number of Internet users in 2009

$\qquad = 1,530 \cdot 10^{6}$

$\qquad = 1.53 \cdot 10^{9}$

$\qquad$ Number of Internet users in 2010

$\qquad = 1,650 \cdot 10^{6}$

$\qquad = 1.65 \cdot 10^{9}$

$\qquad$ Total number of Internet users in the 3 years

$\qquad = 1.4 \cdot 10^{9} + 1.53 \cdot 10^{9} + 1.65 \cdot 10^{9}$

$\qquad = (1.4 + 1.53 + 1.65) \cdot 10^{9}$

$\qquad = 4.58 \cdot 10^{9}$

$\qquad$ Average number of Internet users in the 3 years

$\qquad = \dfrac{4.58 \cdot 10^{9}}{3}$

$\qquad \approx 1.5 \cdot 10^{9}$

c) Number of Internet users in 2005
$$= 1{,}018 \cdot 10^6$$
$$= 1.018 \cdot 10^9$$

$$\dfrac{\text{Number of Internet users in 2010}}{\text{Number of Internet users in 2005}}$$

$$= \dfrac{1.65 \cdot 10^9}{1.018 \cdot 10^9}$$

$$= \dfrac{1.65}{1.018} \cdot \dfrac{10^9}{10^9}$$

$$\approx 1.6$$

The number of Internet users in 2010 was 1.6 times as many as the number of Internet users in 2005.

Chapter 3

1. Let the measure of the smallest angle be $x°$.
$$x + x + 9.2 + 2.5x - 30.8 = 180$$
$$4.5x - 21.6 = 180$$
$$4.5x - 21.6 + 21.6 = 180 + 21.6$$
$$4.5x = 201.6$$
$$\dfrac{4.5x}{4.5} = \dfrac{201.6}{4.5}$$
$$x = 44.8$$
$$x + 9.2 = 44.8 + 9.2$$
$$= 54$$
$$2.5x - 30.8 = 2.5(44.8) - 30.8$$
$$= 81.2$$

The measures of the three angles are 44.8°, 54°, and 81.2°.

2. Let the speed of the slower yacht be x miles per hour.
So, $(x + 6)$ miles per hour is the speed of the faster yacht.

$$\dfrac{1}{3}x + \dfrac{1}{3}(x + 6) = 39$$

$$\dfrac{1}{3}x + \dfrac{1}{3}x + \dfrac{6}{3} = 39$$

$$\dfrac{2}{3}x + 2 = 39$$

$$\dfrac{2}{3}x + 2 - 2 = 39 - 2$$

$$\dfrac{2}{3}x = 37$$

$$\dfrac{2}{3}x \cdot \dfrac{3}{2} = 37 \cdot \dfrac{3}{2}$$

$$x = 55.5$$

$$x + 6 = 55.5 + 6$$

$$= 61.5$$

The speeds of the two yachts are 55.5 and 61.5 miles per hour.

3. a) Let the length of the longest piece of ribbon be x feet.
So, the length of the shortest piece of ribbon is $\dfrac{2}{3}x$ feet.

$$x + \dfrac{2}{3}x + \left(x - 1\dfrac{3}{4}\right) = \dfrac{8}{3}x - \left(\dfrac{7}{4}\right)$$

$$2\dfrac{2}{3}x - 1\dfrac{3}{4} = \dfrac{8}{3}x - \dfrac{7}{4}$$

$$\dfrac{8}{3}x - \dfrac{7}{4} = \dfrac{8}{3}x - \dfrac{7}{4}$$

Because $\dfrac{8}{3}x - \dfrac{7}{4} = \dfrac{8}{3}x - \dfrac{7}{4}$ is always true, the linear equation is true for any value of x. So, this equation has infinitely many solutions. So, she cannot find the length of each piece of ribbon.

b)
$$x + \dfrac{2}{3}x + x - 1\dfrac{3}{4} = 22\dfrac{1}{4}$$

$$\dfrac{8}{3}x - \dfrac{7}{4} = 22\dfrac{1}{4}$$

$$\dfrac{8}{3}x - \dfrac{7}{4} + \dfrac{7}{4} = \dfrac{89}{4} + \dfrac{7}{4}$$

$$\dfrac{8}{3}x = 24$$

$$\dfrac{8}{3}x \cdot \dfrac{3}{8} = 24 \cdot \dfrac{3}{8}$$

$$x = 9$$

$$\dfrac{2}{3}x = \dfrac{2}{3}(9)$$

$$= 6$$

$$x - 1\dfrac{3}{4} = 9 - 1\dfrac{3}{4}$$

$$= 7\dfrac{1}{4}$$

She can find the length of each piece of ribbon now because the equation has one solution. The lengths of the three pieces of ribbons are 9 feet, $7\dfrac{1}{4}$ feet, and 6 feet.

4. a) Let the distance James travels uphill be d miles.
So, $(18 - d)$ miles is the distance he travels downhill.
A linear equation for the distance he travels is $\dfrac{d}{4} + \dfrac{(18 - d)}{6} = 4$.

b)

$$\frac{d}{4} + \frac{(18 - d)}{6} = 4$$

$$\frac{d}{4} \cdot 12 + \frac{(18 - d)}{6} \cdot 12 = 4 \cdot 12$$

$$3d + 2(18 - d) = 48$$
$$3d + 36 - 2d = 48$$
$$d + 36 = 48$$
$$d + 36 - 36 = 48 - 36$$
$$d = 12$$
$$18 - d = 18 - 12$$
$$= 6$$

He travels 6 miles downhill.

c) Time he takes to pedal uphill $= \frac{d}{4}$

$$= \frac{12}{4}$$

$$= 3 \text{ h}$$

Time he takes to ride downhill $= \frac{18 - d}{6}$

$$= \frac{6}{6}$$

$$= 1 \text{ h}$$

$3 - 1 = 2$

The difference in time spent pedaling uphill versus riding downhill is 2 hours.

5. a) Casey can install $\frac{1}{20}$ of the fountain in one hour.

Samuel can install $\frac{1}{30}$ of the fountain in one hour.

b) $t \text{ h} \longrightarrow 1$

$1 \text{ h} \longrightarrow \frac{1}{t}$

c)

$$\frac{1}{20} + \frac{1}{30} = \frac{1}{t}$$

$$\frac{1}{20} \cdot 60 + \frac{1}{30} \cdot 60 = \frac{1}{t} \cdot 60$$

$$3 + 2 = \frac{60}{t}$$

$$5 = \frac{60}{t}$$

$$5 \cdot t = \frac{60}{t} \cdot t$$

$$5t = 60$$

$$\frac{5t}{5} = \frac{60}{5}$$

$$t = 12$$

So, they would take a total of 12 hours to install the fountain if they worked together.

6. a) Perimeter of triangle PQR
$$= (x - 3) + (4x + 3) + (3x - 5)$$
$$= (8x - 5) \text{ cm}$$

Perimeter of rectangle $ABCD$

$$= 2\left(4x - \frac{1}{2}\right) + 2(2x + 2)$$

$$= 8x - 1 + 4x + 4$$

$$= (12x + 3) \text{ cm}$$

b)
$$\frac{8x - 5}{12x + 3} = \frac{5}{9}$$

$$9(8x - 5) = 5(12x + 3)$$

$$72x - 45 = 60x + 15$$
$$72x - 45 + 45 = 60x + 15 + 45$$
$$72x = 60x + 60$$
$$72x - 60x = 60x + 60 - 60x$$
$$12x = 60$$
$$\frac{12x}{12} = \frac{60}{12}$$
$$x = 5$$

c) $CD = 2x + 2$
$$= 2(5) + 2$$
$$= 10 + 2$$
$$= 12$$

$BC = 4x - \frac{1}{2}$

$$= 4(5) - \frac{1}{2}$$

$$= 20 - \frac{1}{2}$$

$$= 19.5$$

Area of rectangle $ABCD$

$$= (2x + 2)\left(4x - \frac{1}{2}\right)$$

$$= 12 \cdot 19.5$$

$$= 234 \text{ cm}^2$$

The area of rectangle $ABCD$ is 234 square centimeters.

7. a) $m = 4 + 3(n - 1)$
$$= 4 + 3n - 3$$
$$= 3n + 1$$

b)

Number of Squares (n)	1	2	3	4	5	...	10
Number of Paper Clips (m)	4	7	10	13	16	...	31

© Marshall Cavendish International (Singapore) Private Limited.

c) $m = 3(40) + 1$

$\quad = 120 + 1$

$\quad = 121$

So, 121 paper clips are needed to form 40 squares.

d)
$$80 = 3n + 1$$
$$80 - 1 = 3n + 1 - 1$$
$$79 = 3n$$
$$\frac{3n}{3} = \frac{79}{3}$$
$$n = 26\frac{1}{3}$$

So, Jimmy can form 26 squares, with 1 leftover paper clip.

8. a) Mass of flour $= \dfrac{12.6}{w}$

Mass of ground coffee $= \dfrac{27}{6w}$

$\qquad\qquad\qquad\quad = \dfrac{4.5}{w}$

b) $\dfrac{12.60}{w} + \dfrac{4.5}{w} = 9.5$

c)
$$\frac{12.6}{w} + \frac{4.5}{w} = 9.5$$
$$\frac{12.6}{w} \cdot w + \frac{4.5}{w} \cdot w = 9.5 \cdot w$$
$$12.6 + 4.5 = 9.5w$$
$$9.5w = 17.1$$
$$\frac{9.5w}{9.5} = \frac{17.1}{9.5}$$
$$w = 1.8$$
$$6w = 6(1.8)$$
$$= 10.8$$

So, the price of flour is \$1.80 per pound and the price of ground coffee is \$10.80 per pound.

9. a)
$$V = \frac{1}{3}Bh$$
$$V \cdot 3 = \frac{1}{3}Bh \cdot 3$$
$$3V = Bh$$
$$\frac{3V}{B} = \frac{Bh}{A}$$
$$h = \frac{3V}{B}$$

b) Area of square base $= 10 \cdot 10$

$\qquad\qquad\qquad\qquad = 100 \text{ cm}^2$

When $V = 400$ and $B = 100$,

$$h = \frac{3(400)}{100}$$
$$= \frac{1,200}{100}$$
$$= 12$$

The height of the pyramid is 12 centimeters.

c) Let the slant height of the pyramid be L.
By Pythagorean Theorem,
$$L^2 = 12^2 + 5^2$$
$$L^2 = 144 + 25$$
$$L^2 = 169$$
$$L = \sqrt{169}$$
$$L = 13 \text{ cm}$$

Surface area of pyramid
= Area of four triangles + Base area
$$= 4\left(\frac{1}{2} \cdot 5 \cdot 12\right) + (10 \cdot 10)$$
$$= 4(30) + 100$$
$$= 120 + 100$$
$$= 220 \text{ cm}^2$$

The surface area of the pyramid is 220 square centimeters.

10. Brain@Work
$$QS = 2\left(\frac{8}{x+1}\right)$$
$$= \frac{16}{x+1} \text{ in.}$$

Area of triangle $MQS = \dfrac{1}{2} \cdot QS \cdot MR$

$$= \frac{1}{2}\left(\frac{16}{x+1}\right)(3x-2) \text{ cm}^2$$

$$\frac{1}{2}\left(\frac{16}{x+1}\right)(3x-2) = 14$$
$$\frac{8(3x-2)}{x+1} = 14$$
$$8(3x-2) = 14(x+1)$$
$$24x - 16 = 14x + 14$$
$$24x - 16 + 16 = 14x + 14 + 16$$
$$24x = 14x + 30$$
$$24x - 14x = 14x + 30 - 14x$$
$$10x = 30$$
$$x = 3$$

$NP = 3x - 2 = 3(3) - 2$

$\qquad\qquad = 9 - 2$

$\qquad\qquad = 7$

Area of $MNPR = 7(7)$

$\qquad\qquad\quad = 49 \text{ cm}^2$

Area of triangle $MQR = \dfrac{14}{2}$

$\qquad\qquad\qquad\quad = 7 \text{ cm}^2$

Area of $MNPQ = 49 - 7$

$\qquad\qquad\qquad = 42 \text{ cm}^2$

The area of $MNPQ$ is 42 square centimeters.

11. Brain@Work

a)

$M = 80 + \dfrac{15n}{100}$

$\quad = 80 + \dfrac{15(360)}{100}$

$\quad = 80 + \dfrac{5,400}{100}$

$\quad = 80 + 54$

$\quad = 134$

1 week $\longrightarrow$ $134

4 weeks $\longrightarrow$ $134 \cdot 4 = $536

She receives $536.

b) When $M = 140$,

$140 = 80 + \dfrac{15n}{100}$

$140 - 80 = 80 + \dfrac{15n}{100} - 80$

$\dfrac{15n}{100} = 60$

$\dfrac{15n}{100} \cdot 100 = 60 \cdot 100$

$15n = 6,000$

$\dfrac{15n}{15} = \dfrac{6,000}{15}$

$n = 400$

She advised 400 customers that week.

c) $M = 65 + \dfrac{21n}{100}$

d)

$80 + \dfrac{15n}{100} = 65 + \dfrac{21n}{100}$

$80 + \dfrac{15n}{100} - \dfrac{15n}{100} = 65 + \dfrac{21n}{100} - \dfrac{15n}{100}$

$80 = 65 + \dfrac{6n}{100}$

$80 - 65 = 65 + \dfrac{6n}{100} - 65$

$15 = \dfrac{6n}{100}$

$\dfrac{6n}{100} \cdot 100 = 15 \cdot 100$

$6n = 1,500$

$\dfrac{6n}{6} = \dfrac{1,500}{6}$

$n = 250$

She would have to advise 250 customers in a week.

Chapter 4

1. Write the equation $x = -\dfrac{1}{4}y - 3$ in slope-intercept form.

$4x = -y - 12$

$y = -4x - 12$

Compare the equation $y = -4x - 12$ with $y = mx + b$:

Slope: $m = -4$

So, the line parallel to $x = -\dfrac{1}{4}y - 3$ has slope $m = -4$.

Write the equation $\dfrac{x}{3} + \dfrac{y}{2} = 4$ in slope-intercept form.

$2x + 3y = 24$

$3y = -2x + 24$

$y = -\dfrac{2}{3}x + 8$

Compare the equation $y = -4x - 12$ with $y = mx + b$:

y-intercept: $b = 8$

Use the slope $m = -4$ and the y-intercept $b = 8$ to write the equation.

$y = mx + b$

$y = -4x + 8$

So, the equation of the line is $y = -4x + 8$.

2. The line passes through the point (6, 7) and has a slope of $-\dfrac{1}{2}$.

Use the given slope $-\dfrac{1}{2}$, and the values $x = 6$ and $y = 7$ to find the y-intercept.

$y = mx + b$

$7 = -\dfrac{1}{2}(6) + b$

$7 = -3 + b$

$7 + 3 = -3 + b + 3$

$10 = b$

So, the y-intercept is 10.

3. a) The year 2009 corresponds to $t = 0$ and the year 2012 corresponds to $t = 3$.

So, the two points are (0, 900) and (3, 1,500).

b) The line passes through (0, 900) and (3, 1,500).

Slope $m = \dfrac{1,500 - 900}{3 - 0}$

$\quad = \dfrac{600}{3}$

$\quad = 200$

The slope $m = 200$ represents the rate of student enrollment growth. So, the high school's student enrollment increases by 200 students every year.

c) Use the point (0, 900) to find the
y-intercept.
y-intercept: $b = 900$
The line has a slope of 200 and
y-intercept, 900.
$y = mx + b$
$P = 200t + 900$
So, the equation that relates the student
enrollment and the number of years
after 2009 is $P = 200t + 900$.

d) There are 8 years from 2009 to 2017.
Prediction for student enrollment in
2017
$= 200(8) + 900$
$= 2,500$
So, it is likely that 2,500 students will be
enrolled in the school in 2017.

4. a)

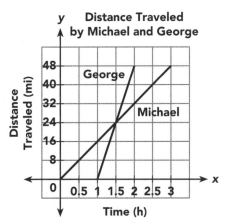

y   **Distance Traveled
by Michael and George**

b) From the graph, the two lines meet
at (1.5, 24). That means George will
pass Michael 1.5 hours after Michael
leaves. So, George will pass Michael
at 10:30 A.M., at a distance of 24 miles
away from Town A.

c) From the graph, George takes 1 hour to
reach Town B and Michael takes 3 hours
to reach Town B. That means if Michael
wants to reach Town B at the same time
as George, he must leave 2 hours earlier
than George. So, Michael must leave at
8:00 A.M.

5. a)

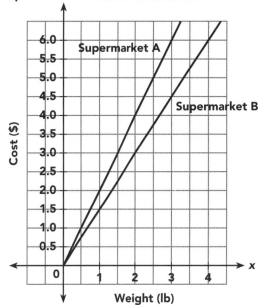

y   **Cost of Strawberries**

b) Supermarket B, because the cost of
strawberries per pound is the slope of
the line. Since the line for Supermarket B
is not as steep as the line for
Supermarket A, the strawberries cost
less at Supermarket B.

6. a) From the graph, the y-intercept of graph
B is 12. It represents the original length
of Candle B.

b) Graph A:
The graph passes through (0, 12) and
(6, 0).
Let (0, 12) be (x_1, y_1) and (6, 0) be (x_2, y_2).

Slope $m = \dfrac{y_2 - y_1}{x_2 - x_1}$

$ = \dfrac{0 - 12}{6 - 0}$

$ = -2$

The line has slope $m = -2$.
The line has a slope of -2 and
y-intercept 12.
$y = mx + b$
$y = -2t + 12$
So, the equation of line A is $y = -2t + 12$.

Graph B:

The graph passes through (0, 12) and
(4, 0).

Let (0, 12) be (x_1, y_1) and (4, 0) be (x_2, y_2).

Slope $m = \dfrac{y_2 - y_1}{x_2 - x_1}$

$ = \dfrac{0 - 12}{4 - 0}$

$ = -3$

The line has slope $m = -3$.
The line has a slope of -3 and y-intercept 12.
$$y = mx + b$$
$$y = -3t + 12$$
So, the equation of line B is $y = -3t + 12$.
Graph C:
The graph passes through $(0, 12)$ and $(2, 0)$.
Let $(0, 12)$ be (x_1, y_1) and $(2, 0)$ be (x_2, y_2).

Slope $m = \dfrac{y_2 - y_1}{x_2 - x_1}$

$ = \dfrac{0 - 12}{2 - 0}$

$ = -6$

The line has slope $m = -6$.
The line has a slope of -6 and y-intercept 12.
$$y = mx + b$$
$$y = -6t + 12$$
So, the equation of line C is $y = -6t + 12$.

c) From the graph, the length of Candle A when $t = 3$ is 6 centimeters.
The length of Candle B when $t = 3$ is 3 centimeters.
So, the two candles were lit 3 hours before x hours.

7. a) Since Alvin is traveling at 60 miles per hour and Town A is 180 miles away from Town B, the slope of the line is -60 and the y-intercept is 180.
So the equation that represents Alvin's distance is $y = -60x + 180$.
Since Megan is traveling at 45 miles per hour and Town A is 180 miles away from Town B, the line has a slope of -45 and y-intercept 180.
So the equation that represents Megan's distance is $y = -45x + 180$.

b)

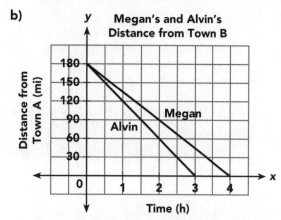

c) Alvin; Alvin is driving faster than Megan so he will reach Town A first.

d) From the graph, Alvin will reach Town A one hour earlier than Megan. So in order for both of them to reach Town A at the same time, Megan would have to leave Town B one hour earlier.

8. a) From the graph, the vertical intercept of the line representing the total price at Studio A is 12.
So, the price of the unpainted vase at Studio A is $12.

b)

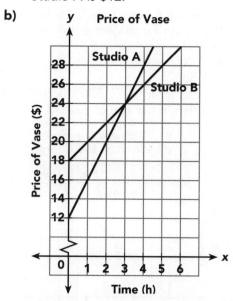

The line representing the total price at Studio A passes through $(0, 12)$ and $(3, 24)$.
Let $(0, 12)$ be (x_1, y_1) and $(3, 24)$ be (x_2, y_2).

Slope $m = \dfrac{y_2 - y_1}{x_2 - x_1}$

$ = \dfrac{24 - 12}{3 - 0}$

$ = \dfrac{12}{3}$

$ = 4$

So, the artist's painting rate at Studio A is $4 per hour.
The line representing the total price at Studio B passes through $(0, 18)$ and $(2, 22)$.
Let $(0, 18)$ be (x_1, y_1) and $(2, 22)$ be (x_2, y_2).

Slope $m = \dfrac{y_2 - y_1}{x_2 - x_1}$

$ = \dfrac{22 - 18}{2 - 0}$

$ = \dfrac{4}{2}$

$ = 2$

So, the artist's painting rate at Studio B is $2 per hour.

c) From the graph, the y values of the graph representing the total price at Studio A is lower than the y values of the graph representing the total price at Studio B when t is less than 3 hours. So, it will be cheaper to buy the vase from Studio A if the painting time needed is less than 3 hours.

9. a) From the graph, Town R is 240 miles away from Town P.

b)

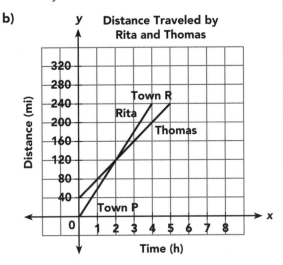

Distance Traveled by Rita and Thomas

c) Rita's graph passes through (0, 0) and (4, 240).
Let (0, 0) be (x_1, y_1) and (4, 240) be (x_2, y_2).

Slope $m = \dfrac{y_2 - y_1}{x_2 - x_1}$

$= \dfrac{240 - 0}{4 - 0}$

$= \dfrac{240}{4}$

$= 60$

The slope represents Rita's driving rate. So, Rita's driving rate is 60 miles per hour. Thomas' graph passes through (0, 40) and (5, 240).
Let (0, 40) be (x_1, y_1) and (5, 240) be (x_2, y_2).

Slope $m = \dfrac{y_2 - y_1}{x_2 - x_1}$

$= \dfrac{240 - 40}{5 - 0}$

$= \dfrac{200}{5}$

$= 40$

The slope represents Thomas' driving rate.
So, Thomas' driving rate is 40 miles per hour.

d) The slope for Rita's graph, $m = 60$.
The y-intercept for Rita's graph, $b = 0$.
The graph that represents Rita's distance from town P, has a slope of 60 and y-intercept 0.
$y = mx + b$
$y = 60x$
So, the equation that represents Rita's distance is $y = 60x$.
The slope for Thomas' graph, $m = 40$.
The y-intercept for Thomas' graph, $b = 40$.
The graph that represents Thomas' distance from town P has a slope of 40 and y-intercept 40.
$y = mx + b$
$y = 40x + 40$
So, the equation that represents Thomas' distance is $y = 40x + 40$.

10. a)

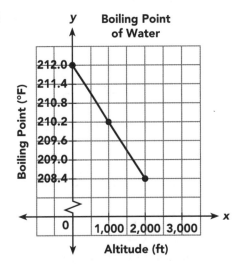

Boiling Point of Water

b) From the graph, the vertical intercept is 212.0.
The boiling point of water at sea level (0 feet altitude) is 212.0°F.

c) The line passes through (0, 212.0) and (1,000, 210.2).
Let (0, 212.0) be (x_1, y_1) and (1,000, 210.2) be (x_2, y_2).

Slope $m = \dfrac{y_2 - y_1}{x_2 - x_1}$

$= \dfrac{210.2 - 212.0}{1,000 - 0}$

$= -\dfrac{1.8}{1,000}$

$= -\dfrac{0.9}{500}$

So, the rate of change of the boiling point of water is −0.9°F per 500 feet.

d) Assuming that the rate of change of the boiling point of water remains constant, let x be the change in boiling point of water at 7,500 feet.

$$-\frac{0.9}{500} = -\frac{x}{7,500}$$
$$x = 13.5$$
$$212.0 - 13.5 = 198.5$$

The predicted boiling point of water at 7,500 feet is 198.5°F.

11. Brain@Work

a) $100x + 200y = 1,800$
  $x + 2y = 18$

b)

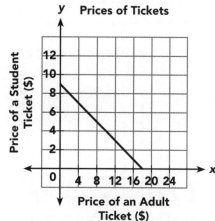

Prices of Tickets

c) y-intercept = 9

It means if the adults do not need to pay, then the price of a student's ticket is $9.00.

d) x-intercept = 18

It means if the students do not need to pay, then the price of an adult's ticket is $18.00.

e) From the graph, the line passes through (10, 4).

That means if students cannot afford to pay more than $4 for a ticket, the adult's ticket must be at least $10.

12. Brain@Work

a) From the graph, the vertical intercept is 3,000.

The fixed cost of producing 500 uniforms per week is $3,000.

b) The line passes through (0, 3,000) and (500, 8,000).

Let (0, 3,000) be (x_1, y_1) and (500, 8,000) be (x_2, y_2).

Slope $m = \dfrac{y_2 - y_1}{x_2 - x_1}$

$\quad = \dfrac{8,000 - 3,000}{500 - 0}$

$\quad = \dfrac{5,000}{500}$

$\quad = 10$

The variable cost of manufacturing 500 uniforms per week is $10 per uniform.

c)

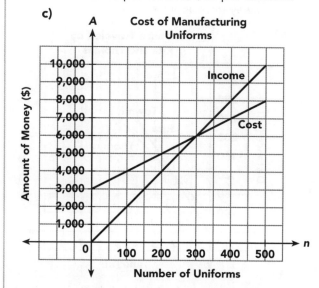

Cost of Manufacturing Uniforms

d) It will be a loss. The graph of cost is above the graph of income when $n = 200$. That means the cost of producing 200 uniforms is more than the profit made from selling the 200 uniforms. So, they will make a loss.

e) The two graphs intersect at $n = 300$, so they must sell 300 uniforms to break even. This means the cost of producing 300 uniforms is the same as the income earned from selling 300 uniforms.

Chapter 5

1. $\dfrac{x}{3} + \dfrac{y}{2} = 4$ — Eq. 1

$\dfrac{2x}{3} - \dfrac{y}{6} = 1$ — Eq. 2

Multiply Eq. 1 by 6:

$6\left(\dfrac{x}{3} + \dfrac{y}{2}\right) = 6 \cdot 4$

$2x + 3y = 24$ — Eq. 3

Multiply Eq. 2 by 6:

$6\left(\dfrac{2x}{3} - \dfrac{y}{6}\right) = 6 \cdot 1$

$4x - y = 6$ — Eq. 4

Multiply Eq. 3 by 2:
$2(2x + 3y) = 2 \cdot 24$
$\quad 4x + 6y = 48$ — Eq. 5
Subtract Eq. 4 from Eq. 5:
$4x + 6y - (4x - y) = 48 - 6$
$\quad 4x + 6y - 4x + y = 42$
$\qquad\qquad\qquad 7y = 42$
$\qquad\qquad\qquad\ y = 6$
Substitute 6 for y into Eq. 4:
$4x - 6 = 6$
$\quad 4x = 6 + 6$
$\quad 4x = 12$
$\quad\ x = 3$
So, the solution of the system of linear equations is $x = 3$ and $y = 6$.

2. $\quad 0.8x - 3y = -6$ — Eq. 1
$\quad 1.2x + 0.5y = 3$ — Eq. 2
Multiply Eq. 1 by 10:
$10(0.8x - 3y) = 10 \cdot (-6)$
$\quad 8x - 30y = -60$
$\quad \dfrac{8x - 30y}{2} = \dfrac{-60}{2}$
$\quad 4x - 15y = -30$ — Eq. 3
Multiply Eq. 2 by 10:
$10(1.2x + 0.5y) = 10 \cdot 3$
$\quad 12x + 5y = 30$ — Eq. 4
Multiply Eq. 3 by 3:
$3(4x - 15y) = 3 \cdot (-30)$
$\quad 12x - 45y = -90$ — Eq. 5
Subtract Eq. 5 from Eq. 4:
$12x + 5y - (12x - 45y) = 30 - (-90)$
$\quad 12x + 5y - 12x + 45y = 30 + 90$
$\qquad\qquad\qquad\quad 50y = 120$
$\qquad\qquad\qquad\qquad y = 2.4$
Substitute 2.4 for y into Eq. 1:
$0.8x - 3(2.4) = -6$
$\quad 0.8x - 7.2 = -6$
$\qquad 0.8x = -6 + 7.2$
$\qquad 0.8x = 1.2$
$\qquad\quad x = 1.5$
So, the solution of the system of linear equations is $x = 1.5$ and $y = 2.4$.

3. Let Mrs. Merlin's present age be x.
Let Josh's present age be y.
$x - 5 = 8(y - 5)$ — Eq. 1
$x + y = 46$ — Eq. 2
Solve for x in terms of y using Eq. 2:
$x = 46 - y$ — Eq. 3
Substitute Eq. 3 into Eq. 1:
$(46 - y) - 5 = 8(y - 5)$
$\quad 46 - y - 5 = 8y - 40$
$46 - 5 + 40 = 8y + y$
$\qquad\qquad 81 = 9y$
$\qquad\qquad\ y = 9$

Substitute 9 for y into Eq. 3:
$x = 46 - 9$
$x = 37$
Mr. Merlin's present age: $37 + 1 = 38$.
Mr. Merlin's age two years from now:
$38 + 2 = 40$.
Mr. Merlin will be 40 years old two years from now.

4. Let the amount of money Steve has be x.
Let the amount of money Ben has be y.
$y + 3 = 2(x - 3)$ — Eq. 1
$y - 7 = \dfrac{1}{3}(x + 7)$ — Eq. 2
Simplify Eq. 1:
$y + 3 = 2x - 6$
$\quad y = 2x - 6 - 3$
$\quad y = 2x - 9$ — Eq. 3
Multiply Eq. 2 by 3:
$3(y - 7) = 3\left[\dfrac{1}{3}(x + 7)\right]$
$3y - 21 = x + 7$
$\quad 3y = x + 7 + 21$
$\quad 3y = x + 28$ — Eq. 4
Substitute Eq. 3 into Eq. 4:
$3(2x - 9) = x + 28$
$\quad 6x - 27 = x + 28$
$\quad 6x - x = 28 + 27$
$\qquad 5x = 55$
$\qquad\ x = 11$
Substitute 11 for x into Eq. 3:
$y = 2(11) - 9$
$y = 13$
So, Steve has $11 in his wallet and Ben has $13 in his wallet.

5. a) Let the price of an adult museum ticket be x.
Let the price of a child museum ticket be y.
$\quad 2x + y = 16.50$ — Eq. 1
$\quad 17x + 8y = 138$ — Eq. 2
Solve for y in terms of x using Eq. 1:
$y = 16.50 - 2x$ — Eq. 3
Substitute Eq. 3 into Eq. 2:
$17x + 8(16.50 - 2x) = 138$
$\quad 17x + 132 - 16x = 138$
$\qquad\quad x + 132 = 138$
$\quad x + 132 - 132 = 138 - 132$
$\qquad\qquad\quad x = 6$
Substitute 6 for x into Eq. 3:
$y = 16.50 - 2(6)$
$y = 4.50$
The price of an adult museum ticket is $6 and the price of a child museum ticket is $4.50.

b) $3x + 12y = 3(6) + 12(4.50)$
$$= 72$$
The total cost of admission tickets for 3 adults and 12 children is $72.

6. Let the average rate of speed of the faster car be y miles per hour.
Let the average rate of speed of the slower car be x miles per hour.

$$y = x + 15 \qquad\qquad\text{— Eq. 1}$$
$$3y + 3x = 375 \qquad\qquad\text{— Eq. 2}$$

Substitute Eq. 1 into Eq. 2:
$$3(x + 15) + 3x = 375$$
$$3x + 45 + 3x = 375$$
$$6x = 375 - 45$$
$$6x = 330$$
$$x = 55$$

Substitute 55 for x into Eq. 1:
$$y = 55 + 15$$
$$y = 70$$

The average rate of speed of the faster car is 70 miles per hour and the average rate of speed of the slower car is 55 miles per hour.

7. Let James' speed be x miles per hour.
Let George's speed be y miles per hour.

$$\frac{36}{60}x + \frac{36}{60}y = 21 \qquad\qquad\text{— Eq. 1}$$
$$7x - 7y = 21 \qquad\qquad\text{— Eq. 2}$$

Simplify Eq. 1:
$$\frac{3}{5}x + \frac{3}{5}y = 21$$
$$5\left(\frac{3}{5}x + \frac{3}{5}y\right) = 5 \cdot 21$$
$$3x + 3y = 105$$
$$\frac{3x + 3y}{3} = \frac{105}{3}$$
$$x + y = 35$$
$$y = 35 - x \qquad\qquad\text{— Eq. 3}$$

Substitute Eq. 3 into Eq. 2:
$$7x - 7(35 - x) = 21$$
$$7x - 245 + 7x = 21$$
$$7x + 7x = 21 + 245$$
$$14x = 266$$
$$x = 19$$

Substitute 19 for x into Eq. 3:
$$y = 35 - 19$$
$$y = 16$$

James' speed is 19 miles per hour and George's speed is 16 miles per hour.

8. Let the numerator be x and the denominator be y.

$$\frac{22 - x}{y} = \frac{1}{3} \qquad\qquad\text{— Eq. 1}$$
$$\frac{1}{5}(x + y) = 8 \qquad\qquad\text{— Eq. 2}$$

Simplify Eq. 1:
$$3(22 - x) = 1(y)$$
$$y = 66 - 3x \qquad\qquad\text{— Eq. 3}$$

Multiply Eq. 2 by 5:
$$5\left[\frac{1}{5}(x + y)\right] = 5 \cdot 8$$
$$x + y = 40 \qquad\qquad\text{— Eq. 4}$$

Substitute Eq. 3 into Eq. 4:
$$x + 66 - 3x = 40$$
$$66 - 2x = 40$$
$$-2x = 40 - 66$$
$$2x = 26$$
$$x = 13$$

Substitute 13 for x into Eq. 3:
$$y = 66 - 3(13)$$
$$y = 66 - 39$$
$$y = 27$$

The original fraction is $\frac{13}{27}$.

9. Let the volume of gold be x cm³.
Let the volume of silver be y cm³.

$$x + y = 8 \qquad\qquad\text{— Eq. 1}$$
$$19x + 10.5y = 92.5 \qquad\qquad\text{— Eq. 2}$$

Solve for x in terms of y using Eq. 1:
$$x = 8 - y \qquad\qquad\text{— Eq. 3}$$

Substitute Eq. 3 into Eq. 2:
$$19(8 - y) + 10.5y = 92.5$$
$$152 - 19y + 10.5y = 92.5$$
$$-8.5y = -59.5$$
$$y = 7$$

The volume of silver is 7 cm³.

Percentage of silver $= \dfrac{7}{8} \cdot 100\%$
$$= 87.5\%$$

87.5% of the necklace is made of silver.

10. Let x milliliters be the volume of Solution A.
Let y milliliters be the volume of Solution B.

$$x + y = 150 \qquad\qquad\text{— Eq. 1}$$
$$0.3x + 0.8y = 0.7(150) \qquad\qquad\text{— Eq. 2}$$

Simplify Eq. 2:
$$0.3x + 0.8y = 105$$
$$10(0.3x + 0.8y) = 10 \cdot 105$$
$$3x + 8y = 1{,}050 \qquad\qquad\text{— Eq. 3}$$

Solve for y in terms of x using Eq. 1:
$$y = 150 - x \qquad\qquad\text{— Eq. 4}$$

Substitute Eq. 4 into Eq. 3:
$$3x + 8(150 - x) = 1{,}050$$
$$3x + 1{,}200 - 8x = 1{,}050$$
$$-5x = -150$$
$$x = 30$$

Substitute 30 for x into Eq. 4:
$$y = 150 - 30$$
$$y = 120$$

So, 30 milliliters of Solution A and 120 milliliters of Solution B are used to create the 70% acid solution.

© Marshall Cavendish International (Singapore) Private Limited.

11. a) $C = 12 + 8n$
$C = 10n$

b) **Payment Options of Fitness Club**

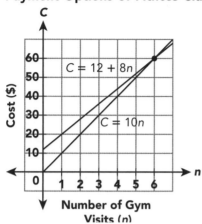

c) From the graph, it would be beneficial to be a member after 6 gym visits.

12. a) Let the cost of a party hat be h.
Let the cost of a balloon be b.
$40h + 10b = 13.20$ — Eq. 1
$20h + 5b = 6.60$ — Eq. 2

b) Multiply Eq. 2 by 2:
$2(20h + 5b) = 2 \cdot 6.60$
$40h + 10b = 13.20$
Since Eq. 1 and Eq. 2 are equivalent, they have an infinite number of solutions. You cannot find the cost of one party hat and one balloon because the system of equations is dependent.

c) $8h + 4b = 2.88$ — Eq. 3
Divide Eq. 3 by 4:
$\dfrac{8h + 4b}{4} = \dfrac{2.88}{4}$
$2h + b = 0.72$
$b = 0.72 - 2h$ — Eq. 4
Substitute Eq. 4 into Eq. 2:
$20h + 5(0.72 - 2h) = 6.60$
$20h + 3.6 - 10h = 6.60$
$10h + 3.6 = 6.6$
$10h + 3.6 - 3.6 = 6.6 - 3.6$
$10h = 3$
$\dfrac{10h}{10} = \dfrac{3}{10}$
$h = 0.30$
Substitute 0.30 for h into Eq. 4:
$b = 0.72 - 2(0.30)$
$b = 0.12$
You can use this information to find the cost of one party hat and the cost of one balloon because the system of linear equations has one unique solution.

13. Brain@Work
Let the tens digit of the original two-digit number be x and the ones digit be y.
Since the ones digit of the original number is bigger than the tens digit, the new two-digit number is greater than the original two-digit number.
$10x + y = 10y + x - 54$ — Eq. 1
$y = 2x + 3$ — Eq. 2
Simplify Eq. 1:
$10x + y = 10y + x - 54$
$10x - x = 10y - y - 54$
$9x = 9y - 54$
$x = y - 6$ — Eq. 3
Substitute Eq. 3 into Eq. 2:
$y = 2(y - 6) + 3$
$y = 2y - 12 + 3$
$y = 2y - 9$
$-y = -9$
$y = 9$
Substitute 9 for y into Eq. 3:
$x = 9 - 6$
$x = 3$
The original two-digit number is 39.

14. Brain@Work
a) $4x + 6y + 10z = 620$ — Eq. 1
$6x + 8y + 10z = 740$ — Eq. 2
Divide Eq. 1 by 2:
$\dfrac{4x + 6y + 10z}{2} = \dfrac{620}{2}$
$2x + 3y + 5z = 310$ — Eq. 3
Divide Eq. 2 by 2:
$\dfrac{6x + 8y + 10z}{2} = \dfrac{740}{2}$
$3x + 4y + 5z = 370$ — Eq. 4
Subtract Eq. 3 from Eq. 4:
$3x + 4y + 5z - (2x + 3y + 5z)$
$= 370 - 310$
$3x + 4y + 5z - 2x - 3y - 5z = 60$
$x + y = 60$
Possible solution 1: $x = 20$, $y = 40$
Substitute 20 for x and 40 for y into Eq. 3:
$2(20) + 3(40) + 5z = 310$
$160 + 5z = 310$
$5z = 310 - 160$
$5z = 150$
$z = 30$
Possible solution 2: $x = 25$, $y = 35$
Substitute 25 for x and 35 for y into Eq. 3:
$2(25) + 3(35) + 5z = 310$
$155 + 5z = 310$
$5z = 310 - 155$
$5z = 155$
$z = 31$

The two possible sets of solutions are $x = 20$, $y = 40$, $z = 30$, and $x = 25$, $y = 35$, $z = 31$.

b) No, the answers for **a)** are not the only possible solutions. Any whole number values of x and y that satisfy the equation $x + y = 60$ can also be solutions.

Chapter 6

1. a)

Figure Number (n input)	1	2	3	4
Number of Dots (D output)	5	8	11	14

b) One-to-one relation

c) Yes, it is a function because for every input value there is only one output value.
$D = 5 + (n - 1) \cdot 3$
$D = 5 + 3n - 3$
$D = 3n + 2$
The equation is $D = 3n + 2$.

2. a) $P = 7.5n - 300$

b) The domain represents the number n of baseball caps sold. The range represents the profit made on selling n baseball caps.

c) When $n = 0$, $p = -300$
When $n = 20$, $p = 7.5(20) - 300$
$\qquad\qquad\qquad = -150$
When $n = 30$, $p = 7.5(30) - 300$
$\qquad\qquad\qquad = -75$
When $n = 40$, $p = 7.5(40) - 300$
$\qquad\qquad\qquad = 0$
When $n = 50$, $p = 7.5(50) - 300$
$\qquad\qquad\qquad = 75$
The range is $\{-300, -150, -75, 0, 75\}$.
The store will begin making a profit when they sell more than 40 baseball caps.

3. a) $D = -1,200 + 15t$

b)

t	D
0	−1,200
10	−1,050
20	−900
30	−750
40	−600
50	−450

c)

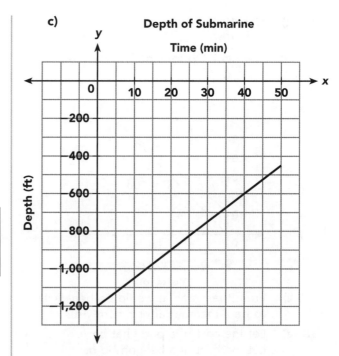

Depth of Submarine

d) **Method 1**
Extend the line until it intersects the horizontal axis and read the corresponding time at that point.
$t = 80$ min

Method 2
$-1,200 + 15t = 0$
$-1,200 + 1,200 + 15t = 0 + 1,200$
$\qquad\qquad\quad 15t = 1,200$
$\qquad\qquad\qquad t = 80$ min
It will take 80 minutes for the submarine to reach the surface of the water.

4. a) $y = 30 + 0.25x$

b)

x	0	40	80	100	140
y	30	40	50	55	65

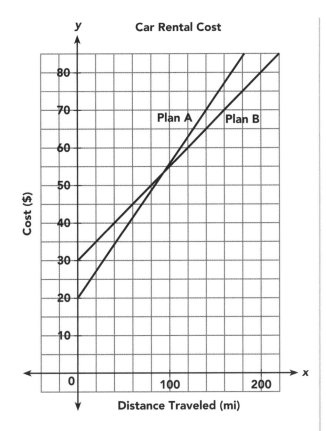

Car Rental Cost

Cost ($)

Distance Traveled (mi)

6. a)

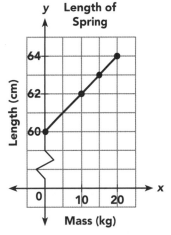

Length of Spring

Length (cm)

Mass (kg)

b) Vertical intercept = 60
The graph passes through (0, 60) and (20, 64).

Slope $m = \dfrac{y_2 - y_1}{x_2 - x_1}$

$= \dfrac{64 - 60}{20 - 0}$

$= 0.2$

The vertical intercept is the original length of the spring. The slope of the graph is the length that the spring stretches per kilogram.

c) $y = 0.2x + 60$

d) **Method 1**
From the graph, $y = 68$ when $x = 40$.

Method 2
Substitute 40 for x into the equation:
$y = 0.2x + 60$
$y = 0.2(40) + 60$
$y = 68$
The spring will be 68 centimeters long.

c) The total charges from Plan A includes a $20 fixed payment plus 35¢ a mile; whereas Plan B charges a $30 fixed payment plus 25¢ a mile. From the graph, Plan A is cheaper when x is less than 100; thus it is better to use Plan A if the car is driven less than 100 miles. If the car is to be driven for more than 100 miles, then Plan B is better.

d) The two plans cost the same when the car is driven 100 miles.

5. a) $P = 12x + 5$

b) $Q = P + 0.4P$
   $= 12x + 5 + 0.4(12x + 5)$
   $= 12x + 5 + 4.8x + 2$
   $= 16.8x + 7$

c) $Q = 16.8(0.05) + 7$
   $= 7.84$
   The retail price of a case of 12 CD boxes is $7.84.

7. a) (3,000, 1,400) and (1,000, 600)

b)

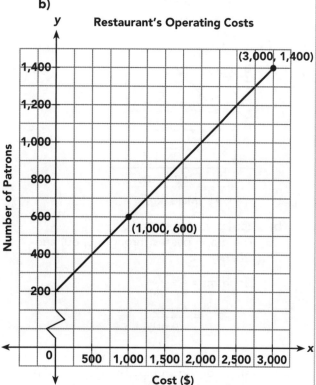

Restaurant's Operating Costs

c) The line passes through (3,000, 1,400) and (1,000, 600).

Slope $m = \dfrac{y_2 - y_1}{x_2 - x_1}$

$= \dfrac{1,400 - 600}{3,000 - 1,000}$

$= \dfrac{800}{2,000}$

$= \dfrac{2}{5}$

The graph passes through the y-axis at (0, 200). So, the y-intercept b is 200. The equation for the function is $C = \dfrac{2}{5}n + 200$.

d) The graph passes through (250, 300). So, the operating cost is $300 with only 250 monthly patrons.

8. a) Patricia's function: $y = 60 - 2x$
Veronica's function: $y = 40 + 3x$

b) Patricia's function is a decreasing linear function with an initial output value of 60 that corresponds to an input value of 0. Veronica's function is an increasing linear function with an initial output value of 40 that corresponds to an input value of 0. Since $60 > 40$, Patricia has a greater amount of money

at first. Comparing the rates of change show that Patricia's saving decreases by $2 each week; and Veronica's saving increases by $3 each week.

c)

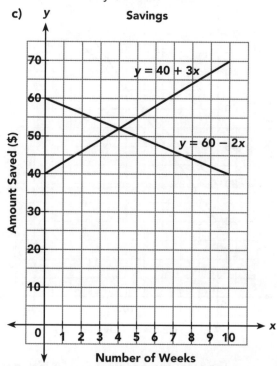

Savings

$y = 40 + 3x$

$y = 60 - 2x$

d) The graphs intersect at $x = 4$. This means that after 4 weeks, the two sisters will have the same amount of money.

9. a)

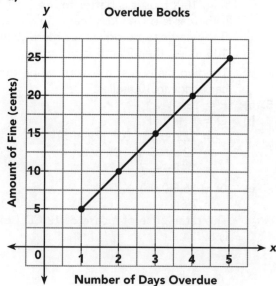

Overdue Books

The points on the graph should not be connected, as the number of books can only be whole numbers. This is a one-to-one relation. It is a function as there is only one output value for every input value.

10.

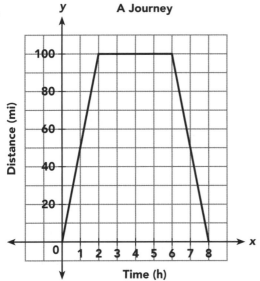

A Journey

The points on the graph should be connected, as both time and distance are continuous data. This is a many-to-one relation. It is a function as every input value has only one output value.

11.

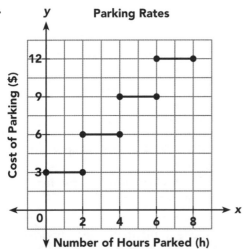

Parking Rates

The points on the graph should only be connected for every 2-hour interval, as the data is continuous within these intervals. This is a many-to-one relation. It is a function as every input value has only one output value.

12. a)

Length of Side (*x* inches)	1	$1\frac{1}{2}$	2	$2\frac{1}{2}$	3
Perimeter (*P* inches)	4	6	8	10	12
Area (*A* square inches)	1	$2\frac{1}{4}$	4	$6\frac{1}{4}$	9

b)

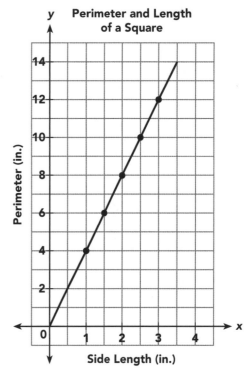

Perimeter and Length of a Square

c)

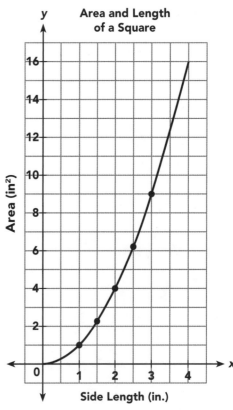

Area and Length of a Square

d) The function for the perimeter is linear and the function for the area is nonlinear.

13. Brain@Work

a) $C(x) = x - 150$

b) $D(x) = 0.8x$

c) $C(D(x)) = 0.8x - 150$

d) $D(C(x)) = 0.8(x - 150)$
$\qquad\qquad\quad = 0.8x - 120$

e) $C(D(x)) = 0.8x - 150$
$\qquad\qquad\quad = 0.8(2,000) - 150$
$\qquad\qquad\quad = \$1,450$

$\quad\ D(C(x)) = 0.8x - 120$
$\qquad\qquad\quad = 0.8(2,000) - 120$
$\qquad\qquad\quad = \$1,480$

Taking the discount first is most advantageous to the customer as it results in the greatest savings.

14. Brain@Work

a) Since E varies directly as the square of its speed v,
$E = kv^2$ where k is a constant

$\text{Constant of proportionality} = \dfrac{E}{v^2}$

$\qquad\qquad\qquad\qquad\qquad\ = \dfrac{140}{2^2}$

$\qquad\qquad\qquad\qquad\qquad\ = 35$

The equation is $E = 35v^2$.

b) When $v = 5$ m/s, $E = 35(5)v^2$
$\qquad\qquad\qquad\qquad\quad = 875$ J

c) $E = 35v^2$

$\dfrac{E}{35} = \dfrac{35v^2}{35}$

$\dfrac{E}{35} = v^2$

$\sqrt{\dfrac{E}{35}} = v$

$v = \sqrt{\dfrac{E}{35}}$

Chapter 7

1. In $\triangle CEF$, $CF^2 = CE^2 + EF^2$
$\qquad\qquad\quad 20^2 = CE^2 + 15.3^2$
$\qquad\qquad\ CE^2 = 20^2 - 15.3^2$
$\qquad\qquad\ CE^2 = 400 - 234.09$
$\qquad\qquad\ CE^2 = 165.91$
$\qquad\qquad\quad CE \approx 12.88$
$DE = DF - EF$
$DE = 19.6 - 15.3$
$DE = 4.3$
So, $BC = DE = 4.3$.
In $\triangle ABC$, $AC^2 = AB^2 + BC^2$
$\qquad\qquad\quad 10^2 = AB^2 + 4.3^2$
$\qquad\qquad\ 100 = AB^2 + 18.49$

$\qquad\qquad AB^2 = 100 - 18.49$
$\qquad\qquad AB^2 = 81.51$
$\qquad\qquad\ AB \approx 9.03$
$AD = AB + BD$
$\quad\ = 9.03 + 12.88$
$\quad\ \approx 21.9$
The length of $\overline{AD}$ is about 21.9 inches.

2. a) Let x be the length of Mr. Jackson's lawn.
So, the area of Mr. Jackson's lawn is x square feet.
$x^2 = 8^2 + 4^2$
$x^2 = 64 + 16$
$x^2 = 80$
The area of Mr. Jackson's lawn is 80 square feet.
Let y be the length of Mr. Smith's lawn.
So, the area of Mr. Smith's lawn is y square feet.
$10^2 = 3^2 + y^2$
$100 = 9 + y^2$
$\quad\ y^2 = 100 - 9$
$\quad\ y^2 = 91$
The area of Mr. Smith's lawn is 91 square feet.
Mr. Smith has a greater area of lawn.

b) Length of fences required for Mr. Jackson's lawn
$= 8.94 + 8.94 + 8.94 + 4 + 8$
$= 38.8$ ft
Length of fence required for Mr. Smith's lawn
$= 9.54 + 9.54 + (9.54 - 3) + 10$
$= 35.6$ ft
Mr. Smith's lawn requires the least amount of fencing.

3. To identify which wing options are right triangles, use the Pythagorean Theorem.
Wing A: $\qquad\quad 39^2 = 1,521$
$\qquad\quad 15^2 + 36^2 = 1,521$
$\qquad\quad$ So, $39^2 = 15^2 + 36^2$
Wing A is a right triangle.
Wing B: $\qquad\quad 27^2 = 729$
$\qquad\qquad 8^2 + 25^2 = 689$
$\qquad\qquad$ So, $27^2 \neq 8^2 + 25^2$
Wing B is not a right triangle.
Wing C: $\qquad\quad 41^2 = 1,681$
$\qquad\quad 40^2 + 9^2 = 1,681$
$\qquad\quad$ So, $41^2 = 40^2 + 9^2$
Wing C is a right triangle.
Wing D: $\qquad\quad 60^2 = 3,600$
$\qquad\quad 33^2 + 56^2 = 4,225$
$\qquad\quad$ So, $60^2 \neq 33^2 + 56^2$
Wing D is not a right triangle.
Pedro is considering wing options A or C.

4. Front cover of book: $8^2 = 6^2 + x^2$
$$x^2 = 8^2 - 6^2$$
$$x^2 = 64 - 36$$
$$x^2 = 28$$
$$x \approx 5.3$$
Width of book: $7^2 = x^2 + y^2$
$$y^2 = 7^2 - x^2$$
$$y^2 = 7^2 - 28$$
$$y^2 = 49 - 28$$
$$y^2 = 21$$
$$y \approx 4.6$$
The values of x and y are about 5.3 inches and 4.6 inches.

5. 5,280 ft = 1 mi

$$500 \text{ ft} = \frac{500}{5,280} \approx 0.095 \text{ mi}$$

Jack's route:
$$x^2 \approx 0.095^2 + 0.5^2$$
$$x^2 = 0.259025$$
$$x \approx 0.509 \text{ mile}$$

$$\text{Jack's time} \approx \frac{0.509}{8}$$
$$= 0.063625 \text{ h}$$
$$\approx 3.8 \text{ min}$$

Jill's route:
$$y^2 \approx 0.095^2 + 0.75^2$$
$$y^2 = 0.571525$$
$$y \approx 0.756 \text{ mile}$$

$$\text{Jill's time} \approx \frac{0.756}{10} = 0.0756 \text{ h} \approx 4.5 \text{ min}$$
Jack will reach point C first.

6. Distance between Campsite A and the ranger station
$$= \sqrt{(-6 - 2)^2 + (3 - 1)^2}$$
$$= \sqrt{64 + 4}$$
$$= \sqrt{68}$$
$$\approx 8.25 \text{ units}$$
Distance between Campsite B and the ranger station
$$= \sqrt{(4 - 2)^2 + (7 - 1)^2}$$
$$= \sqrt{4 + 36}$$
$$= \sqrt{40}$$
$$\approx 6.32 \text{ units}$$
Campsite B is closest to the ranger station.

7. Let the distance traveled by the red car after two hours be x.
So, the distance traveled by the blue car after two hours is $2x$ miles.

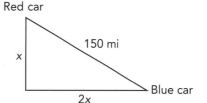
Red car

150 mi

x

Blue car

$2x$

$$x^2 + (2x)^2 = 150^2$$
$$x^2 + 4x^2 = 22,500$$
$$5x^2 = 22,500$$
$$x^2 = 4,500$$
$$x \approx 67.08$$

$$\text{Speed of red car} = \frac{67.08}{2}$$
$$\approx 33.5 \text{ mi/h}$$
$$\text{Speed of blue car} = 2(33.5)$$
$$= 67 \text{ mi/h}$$
The speed of the red car is 33.5 miles per hour and the speed of blue car is 67 miles per hour.

8. Let h represent the height of the cone in inches.
$$5^2 = 3^2 + h^2$$
$$25 = 9 + h^2$$
$$25 - 9 = 9 + h^2 - 9$$
$$h^2 = 16$$
$$h = 4 \text{ in.}$$
Volume of cone
$$= \frac{1}{3}\pi r^2 h$$
$$\approx \frac{1}{3} \cdot 3.14 \cdot 3^2 \cdot 4$$
$$\approx 37.68 \text{ in}^3$$
Volume of cylinder
$$= \pi r^2 h$$
$$\approx 3.14 \cdot 3^2 \cdot 7.5$$
$$= 211.95 \text{ in}^3$$
Volume of hemisphere
$$= \frac{1}{2} \cdot \left(\frac{4}{3}\pi r^3\right)$$
$$\approx \frac{1}{2} \cdot \frac{4}{3} \cdot 3.14 \cdot 3^3$$
$$\approx 56.52 \text{ in}^3$$
Volume of model space shuttle
$$= 37.68 + 211.95 + 56.52$$
$$\approx 306.2 \text{ in}^3$$
The volume of the model space shuttle is 306.2 cubic inches.

9. Let h_1 represent the height of the larger cone in inches.
$$7.8^2 = 4.5^2 + h_1{}^2$$
$$60.84 = 20.25 + h_1{}^2$$
$$60.84 - 20.25 = 20.25 + h_1{}^2 - 20.25$$
$$h_1{}^2 = 40.59$$
$$h_1 \approx 6.37 \text{ in.}$$

Let h_2 represent the height of the small cone in inches.
$$3^2 = 1.5^2 + h_2{}^2$$
$$9 = 2.25 + h_2{}^2$$
$$9 - 2.25 = 2.25 + h_2{}^2 - 2.25$$
$$h_2{}^2 = 6.75$$
$$h_2 \approx 2.60 \text{ in.}$$

Volume of big cone
$$= \frac{1}{3}\pi r^2 h_1$$
$$\approx \frac{1}{3} \cdot 3.14 \cdot 4.5^2 \cdot 6.37$$
$$\approx 135.01 \text{ in}^3$$

Volume of small cone
$$= \frac{1}{3}\pi r^2 h_2$$
$$\approx \frac{1}{3} \cdot 3.14 \cdot 1.5^2 \cdot 2.60$$
$$\approx 6.12 \text{ in}^3$$

Volume of wedge
$$\approx 135.01 - 6.12$$
$$\approx 128.9 \text{ in}^3$$
The volume of the wedge is 128.9 cubic inches.

10. Volume of cylinder
$$= \pi r^2 h$$
$$\approx 3.14 \cdot \left(\frac{0.4}{2}\right)^2 \cdot 1.2$$
$$\approx 0.15 \text{ in}^3$$

Volume of cone $\approx 4.92 - 0.15$
$$\frac{1}{3}\pi r^2 h = 4.77$$
$$\frac{1}{3} \cdot 3.14 \cdot r^2 \cdot 1.45 \approx 4.77$$
$$\frac{1}{3} \cdot 4.553 \cdot r^2 = 4.77$$
$$3 \cdot \frac{1}{3} \cdot 4.553 \cdot r^2 = 4.77 \cdot 3$$
$$4.553 \cdot r^2 = 14.31$$
$$\frac{4.553 \cdot r^2}{4.553} = \frac{14.31}{4.553}$$
$$r^2 = \frac{14.31}{4.553}$$
$$r^2 = \sqrt{\frac{14.31}{4.553}}$$
$$r \approx 1.77$$

Diameter of cone $\approx 1.77 \cdot 2$
$$x \approx 3.5 \text{ in.}$$
The value of x is about 3.5 inches.
$$1.45^2 + 1.77^2 = y^2$$
$$5.2354 = y^2$$
$$2.3 \approx y$$
The value of y is about 2.3 inches.

11. Brain@Work

Let the height of each flag be x.

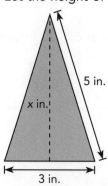

5 in.

x in.

3 in.

$$5^2 = x^2 + 1.5^2$$
$$25 = x^2 + 2.25$$
$$25 - 2.25 = x^2 + 2.25 - 2.25$$
$$x^2 = 22.75$$
$$x = 4.77 \text{ in.}$$
$$1 \text{ ft} = 12 \text{ in.}$$
$$5 \text{ ft} = 5 \cdot 12 = 60 \text{ in.}$$

60 in.

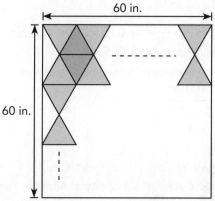

60 in.

There will be one less 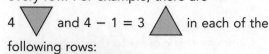 in every row. For example, there are

4 and 4 − 1 = 3 in each of the following rows:

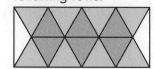

From the length:

First row of = 60 in. ÷ 3 in.
$$= 20 \text{ flags}$$

First row of △ = 20 − 1
= 19 flags

From the width:
60 ÷ 4.77 ≈ 12.58
So, there will be at most 12 rows of flags.
Total number of flags
= (20 + 19) · 12
= 468
She can make 468 flags from the piece of fabric.

12. Brain@Work

a) $r^2 = 1^2 + 1^2$
$r^2 = 1 + 1$
$r^2 = 2$
$r = \sqrt{2}$
$r \approx 1.4$

$s^2 = r^2 + 1^2$
$s^2 = (\sqrt{2})^2 + 1^2$
$s^2 = 2 + 1$
$s = \sqrt{3}$
$s \approx 1.7$

$t^2 = s^2 + 1^2$
$t^2 = (\sqrt{3})^2 + 1^2$
$t^2 = 3 + 1$
$t^2 = 4$
$t^2 = \sqrt{4}$
$t = 2$

$u^2 = t^2 + 1^2$
$u^2 = 4 + 1$
$u^2 = 5$
$u = \sqrt{5}$
$u \approx 2.2$

b) The pattern is $\sqrt{2}, \sqrt{3}, \sqrt{4}, \sqrt{5}...$
$v = \sqrt{6}; w = \sqrt{7}$

Chapter 8

1. 7 units to the left and 8 units down;
(x, y) is mapped onto $(x − 7, y − 8)$

2. a) Scale factor $= \dfrac{6}{2.4} = \dfrac{4.5}{1.8} = 2.5$

b) $6 \cdot \dfrac{1}{3} = 2$

$4.5 \cdot \dfrac{1}{3} = 1.5$

The printed photograph measures 2 inches by 1.5 inches.

3. a) Translation of 4 units to the right.

b) Reflection in the line $x = 4$ or 180° rotation about the point (4, 5), or dilation about (4, 5) with scale factor −1.

c) 90° clockwise rotation about the point (0, 1).

4. a) In 3 hours, the hour hand moves 90°. In 0.5 hour, the hour hand moves
$\dfrac{90°}{3} \cdot 0.5 = 15°$.
90° + 15° = 105°.
The hour hand is rotated 105° clockwise about the origin.

b) (−5, 0)

c) 360° + 180° = 540°

5. a)

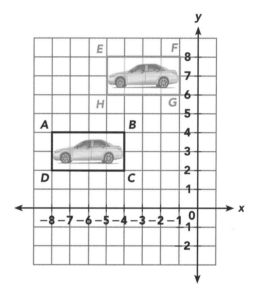

b)

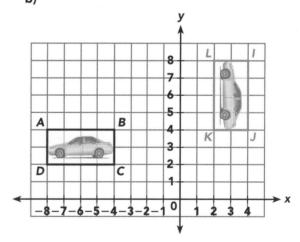

c)

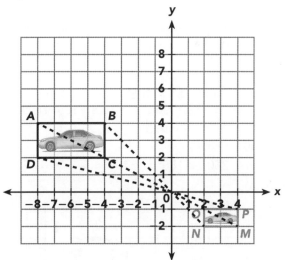

6. a)

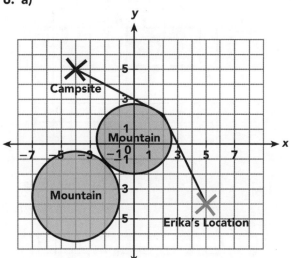

b) A translation of 6 units up and 3 units left followed by another translation of 3 units up and 6 units left.

7. a) Jenny: (−3, 1), Kenny: (3, 2), Lenny: (3, −3), Manny: (−3, −2)

b) Jenny: (−3, −5), Kenny: (3, −6)

c) Jenny: (−5, −3), Kenny: (−6, 3), Lenny: (−1, 3), Manny: (−2, −3)

8. a) The origin is the center of dilation.

Scale factor $= \dfrac{EF}{BC} = \dfrac{16}{8} = 2$

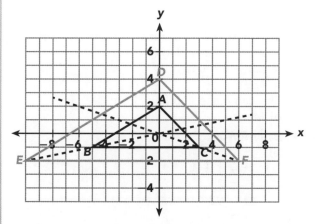

b) J' (4, 6); K' (−4, 0); L' (6, −2)

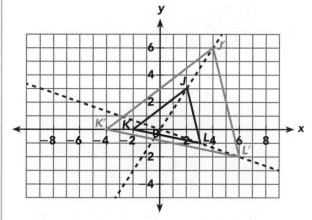

9. a) P (8, 0)

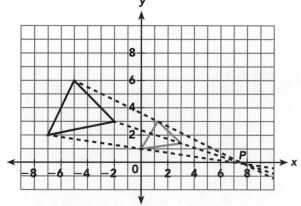

b) Dilation with center (8, 0) and scale factor $-\dfrac{1}{2}$.

10. a) Dilation with center (−5, −1) and scale factor 2.

b)

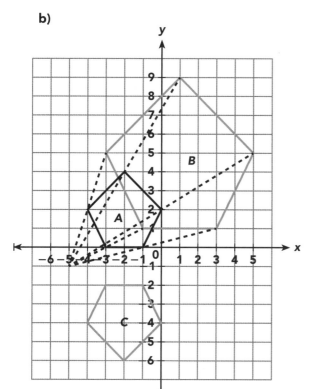

b) $y = -x^2 + 7$

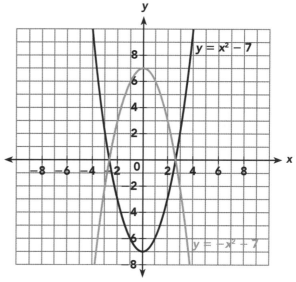

c) Rotate 180° about $(-2, -1)$; Dilation with center $(-2, -1)$ and scale factor -1.

d) Transformation in **a)** preserves the shape of pentagon *A* but the size is increased twice. Both the lengths and angle measures of pentagon *A* are preserved under transformations **b)** and **c)**.

11. a) $y = (x - 3)^2 - 7$

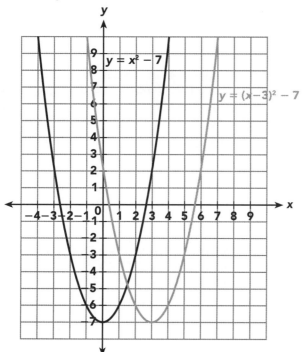

12. a) Go southwest bound on the train for 5 units. Then change trains and go northwest bound for 6 units.

b) From Wellington to Boylston: Go southbound on the train for 4 units. Then go southeast for 1 unit and change trains and go southwest for 3 units. Total number of stations
$= 4 + 3 + 1$
$= 8$
From Wellington to Aquarium: Go southbound on the train for 4 units. Then go southeast for 1 unit and change trains and go southwest for 1 unit. Then change trains again and go southeast for 1 unit and northeast for 1 unit. Total number of stations
$= 4 + 1 + 1 + 1 + 1$
$= 8$
From Wellington to Aquarium, you have to change trains twice. So, even though the number of stations is the same for both journeys, the changing of trains take time. So, it is likely to take more time traveling from Aquarium than from Wellington.

Chapter 9

1. Use the ratio of the areas to find the ratio of corresponding side lengths.

$$k^2 = \frac{\text{Area of } EFGH}{\text{Area of } JKLM}$$

$$k^2 = \frac{10.8}{2.7}$$

$$k = \sqrt{\frac{10.8}{2.7}}$$

$$k = 2$$

Use the ratio of corresponding side lengths to find GH.

$$k = \frac{GH}{LM}$$

$$2 = \frac{GH}{1.5}$$

$$GH = 3$$

Area of $EFGH = 10.8$ cm²

$$GH \cdot GF = 10.8$$

$$3 \cdot GF = 10.8$$

$$GF = \frac{10.8}{3}$$

$$GF = 3.6$$

Since GF is 3 times CE,

$$CE = \frac{3.6}{3}$$

$$= 1.2$$

$$x = CE + GH$$

$$x = 1.2 + 3$$

$$x = 4.2$$

So, the value of x is 4.2 centimeters.

2. a) $\triangle HYD \cong \triangle XGE$

$\overline{XG} \cong \overline{HY}$ [Corr. sides]

$= 1.5$ cm

b) $\triangle HYD \cong \triangle XGE$

$\overline{EG} \cong \overline{DY}$ [Corr. sides]

$= 4.3$ cm

$GY = EY - YD$

$= 6.6 - 4.3$

$= 2.3$ cm

c) $\triangle HYD \cong \triangle XGE$

$\overline{EX} \cong \overline{DH}$ [Corr. sides]

$= 3.6$ cm

$XF = EF - EX$

$= 7 - 3.6$

$= 3.4$ cm

3. a) $m\angle BAC = m\angle BED$ [Corr. $\angle$s; $AC \parallel ED$]

$m\angle ACB = m\angle EDB$ [Corr. $\angle$s; $AC \parallel ED$]

Two pairs of corresponding angles have equal measures. So, $\triangle ABC \sim \triangle EBD$.

b) $\dfrac{\text{Area of } \triangle ABC}{\text{Area of } \triangle EBD} = \dfrac{36}{16}$

So, $\dfrac{EB}{AB} = \dfrac{\sqrt{36}}{\sqrt{16}}$

$$= \frac{6}{4}$$

$$= \frac{3}{2}$$

$$\frac{EB}{AB} = \frac{3}{2}$$

$$\frac{EB}{7} \cdot 7 = \frac{3}{2} \cdot 7$$

$$EB = 10.5$$

The length of $\overline{EB}$ is 10.5 inches.

c) $\dfrac{DB}{CB} = \dfrac{3}{2}$

$$\frac{DB}{5} \cdot 5 = \frac{3}{2} \cdot 5$$

$$DB = 7.5$$

$$CD = BD - BC$$

$$= 7.5 - 5$$

$$= 2.5$$

The length of $\overline{CD}$ is 2.5 inches.

4. Since the triangles are similar, the lengths of their corresponding sides must be in the same ratio.

$$\frac{AB}{DE} = \frac{AC}{DF}$$

$$\frac{7}{10.5} = \frac{2x}{15}$$

$$\frac{7}{10.5} \cdot 15 = \frac{2x}{15} \cdot 15$$

$$10 = 2x$$

$$\frac{10}{2} = \frac{2x}{2}$$

$$5 = x$$

Since the triangles are similar, their corresponding angle measures are equal.

$m\angle Q = m\angle B = 65°$

$m\angle R = 180° - 35° - 65°$ [$\angle$ sum of triangle]

$= 80°$

$m\angle R = z = 80°$

$$m\angle F = m\angle R$$

$$180° - y° = 80°$$

$$180° - y° - 180° = 80° - 180°$$

$$-y = -100$$

$$y = 100$$

The values of x, y, and z are 5, 100, and 80 respectively.

5. Since the two triangles are similar, the lengths of their corresponding sides must be in the same ratio.

$$\frac{AC}{DF} = \frac{AB}{DE}$$

$$\frac{x}{12} = \frac{3}{4.5}$$

$$\frac{x}{12} \cdot 12 = \frac{3}{4.5} \cdot 12$$

$$x = 8$$

Similarly, $\dfrac{BC}{EF} = \dfrac{AB}{DE}$

$$\frac{4 + y}{7 + y} = \frac{3}{4.5}$$

$$4.5(4 + y) = 3(7 + y)$$
$$18 + 4.5y = 21 + 3y$$
$$4.5y - 3y = 21 - 18$$
$$1.5y = 3$$
$$y = \frac{3}{1.5}$$
$$y = 2$$

6. a) Volume of cone $= \dfrac{1}{3}\pi r^2 h$

$$50\pi = \frac{1}{3}\pi r^2(6)$$

$$50\pi = 2\pi r^2$$

$$\frac{2\pi r^2}{2\pi} = \frac{50\pi}{2\pi}$$

$$r^2 = 25$$
$$r = 5$$

The radius of the larger cone is 5 inches.

b) Since the two cones are similar, the corresponding radii and heights must be in the same ratio.
Let the height of the smaller cone be h.

$$\frac{\text{Height of smaller cone}}{\text{Height of bigger cone}} = \frac{\text{Radius of smaller cone}}{\text{Radius of bigger cone}}$$

$$\frac{h}{6} = \frac{1}{5}$$

$$\frac{h}{6} \cdot 6 = \frac{1}{5} \cdot 6$$

$$h = 1.2$$

The height of the smaller cone is 1.3 inches.

c) Volume of water $= \dfrac{1}{3}\pi r^2 h$

$$= \frac{1}{3}\pi(1)^2(1.2)$$

$$= 0.4\pi$$

The greatest volume of water that the smaller cone can hold is 0.4π cubic inches.

d) $\dfrac{\text{Volume of larger cone}}{\text{Volume of smaller cone}} = \dfrac{50}{0.4}$

$$= 125$$

$\dfrac{\text{Height of larger cone}}{\text{Height of smaller cone}} = \dfrac{6}{1.2}$

$$= 5$$

No, the ratios are not the same. The ratio of their volumes is the cube of the ratio of their heights.

7. a) Translation of $\triangle ABC$ 3 units to the right and 3 units up and then dilation of $\triangle A'B'C'$ with center $(-1, 3)$ and scale factor -2.

b) Dilation of $\triangle ABC$ with center $(-3, 1)$ and scale factor -2.

8. A translation of 2 units to the right and then a rotation of 90° clockwise about $(-3, -3)$.

9. Use the ratio of the areas to find the ratio of corresponding lengths.
Actual area of swimming pool
$= 1,250$ m²
$= 12,500,000$ cm²

$$k^2 = \frac{\text{Actual area of swimming pool}}{\text{Area of swimming pool on drawing}}$$

$$k^2 = \frac{12,500,000}{50}$$

$$k = \sqrt{\frac{1,250,000}{5}}$$

$$k = 500$$

Let x be the length of the swimming pool on the scale drawing.

$$\frac{\text{Actual length of swimming pool}}{\text{Length of swimming pool on drawing}} = k$$

$$\frac{5,000}{x} = 500$$

$$x = 10$$

The length of the swimming pool on the map is 10 centimeters.
Map area of swimming pool $= 50$ cm²
$$\text{Length} \cdot \text{Width} = 50$$
$$10 \cdot \text{Width} = 50$$
$$\text{Width} = 5 \text{ cm}$$

Let the diagonal length be y.
Using Pythagorean Theorem,
$$y^2 = 10^2 + 5^2$$
$$y^2 = 100 + 25$$
$$y^2 = 125$$
$$y \approx 11$$

The diagonal length of the swimming pool on the drawing is about 11 centimeters.

© Marshall Cavendish International (Singapore) Private Limited.

10. a) Since *STUVW* is the image of *ABCDE*, the figures are congruent.

$m\angle ACB = m\angle SUT$ [Corr. ∠s]

$m\angle DCE = m\angle VUW$ [Congruent figures]

b) $TU = BC = 3$ in.   [Corr. sides are equal]

The length of $\overline{TU}$ is 3 inches.

$UV = CD = 5$ in.   [Corr. sides are equal]

The length of $\overline{UV}$ is 5 inches.

c) $m\angle CAB = \dfrac{180° - 50°}{2}$ [Isos. triangle]

$\qquad\quad = 65°$

$m\angle ACB = m\angle ECD$ [Vert. opp. ∠s]

$m\angle CED = \dfrac{180° - 50°}{2}$ [Isos. triangle]

$\qquad\quad = 65°$

$m\angle CED = m\angle CAB$

Since there are two pairs of corresponding angles with equal measures, $\triangle ABC \sim \triangle EDC$.

11. Brain@Work

$m\angle A = m\angle D$

$m\angle B = m\angle E$

$m\angle C = m\angle F$

Since there are two pairs of corresponding angles with equal measures, $\triangle ABC \sim \triangle DEF$.

Since $\triangle ABC \sim \triangle DEF$, the lengths of their corresponding sides must be in the same ratio.

$\dfrac{AC}{DF} = \dfrac{AB}{DE}$

$\dfrac{3x}{3} = \dfrac{15}{5}$

$x = 3$

$AC = 3x$

$\quad\;\; = 3(3)$

$\quad\;\; = 9$

In $\triangle ABC$,

$m\angle C = 180° - \angle A - \angle B$

$\qquad\;\; = 180° - 45° - 55°$

$\qquad\;\; = 80°$

$PR = AC = 9$ in.

$QR = BC = 4$ in.

$m\angle R = m\angle C = 80°$

By SAS, $\triangle ABC \cong \triangle PQR$.

Since $\triangle ABC \sim \triangle DEF$, the lengths of their corresponding sides must be in the same ratio.

$\dfrac{EF}{BC} = \dfrac{DE}{AB}$

$\dfrac{z}{4} = \dfrac{5}{15}$

$\dfrac{z}{4} \cdot 4 = \dfrac{5}{15} \cdot 4$

$z = \dfrac{4}{3}$

In $\triangle DEF$,

$m\angle F = m\angle R = 80°$

$\dfrac{PR}{DF} = \dfrac{9}{3} = 3$

$\dfrac{QR}{EF} = 4 \div \dfrac{4}{3}$

$\qquad\;\; = 4 \cdot \dfrac{3}{4}$

$\qquad\;\; = 3$

Since there are two pairs of corresponding side lengths with the same ratio and the included angles have the same measure, $\triangle DEF \sim \triangle PQR$.

So, sails I and III are congruent. Sail II is similar to both sails I and III.

12. Brain@Work

a) $\dfrac{\text{Length of Yasmin's photo}}{\text{Length of Yasmin's frame}} = \dfrac{5}{10} = \dfrac{1}{2}$

$\dfrac{\text{Width of Yasmin's photo}}{\text{Width of Yasmin's frame}} = \dfrac{3}{8}$

Since the ratio of the lengths is not the same as the ratio of the widths, the photograph and the frame are not similar. So, she cannot fit the photograph into the frame without cropping.

b) $\dfrac{\text{Length of Jessica's photo}}{\text{Length of Jessica's frame}} = \dfrac{3}{10}$

$\dfrac{\text{Width of Jessica's photo}}{\text{Width of Jessica's frame}} = \dfrac{3}{10}$

Since there are two pairs of corresponding side lengths with the same ratio, the photograph and frame are similar. So, she can fit her photo in the frame without cropping.

$\dfrac{\text{Length of Jessica's photo}}{\text{Length of Yasmin's frame}} = \dfrac{3}{10}$

$\dfrac{\text{Width of Jessica's photo}}{\text{Width of Yasmin's frame}} = \dfrac{3}{8}$

Since the ratio of the corresponding lengths is not the same as the ratio of the corresponding widths, Jessica's photograph cannot fit into Yasmin's frame without cropping.

c) In order for the photograph to be able to fit into the frame without cropping, the photo frame and the photograph must be similar.

Length of frame: $8 \cdot 2 = 16$

Width of frame: $5 \cdot 2 = 10$

Length of frame: $8 \cdot 3 = 24$

Width of frame: $5 \cdot 3 = 15$

So, the two possible sizes of frames are 10-inch by 16-inch and 15-inch by 24-inch.

Chapter 10

1. a)

Altitude and Temperature

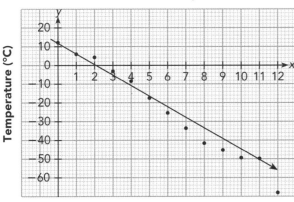

Altitude (km)

c) **Heights and Fertilizer Amounts of Plants**

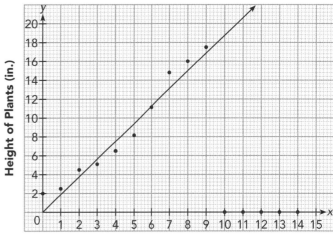

Amount of Fertilizer Used (units/mL)

It is a strong positive linear association between the amount of fertilizer and the height of the plants.

b) There are no outliers.

c) It is a strong and negative linear association. The general trend shows that as the altitude above the Earth's surface increases, the temperature decreases.

d) The line passes through the points (0, 10) and (11, −50).

Slope $m = \dfrac{-50 - 10}{10 - 0}$

$= \dfrac{-60}{11}$

≈ -5.5

The line passes the y-axis at the points (0, 10). So, the y-intercept, b, is 10. The equation for the line of best fit is $Y = -5.5x + 10$.

d) From the line of best fit, the minimum amount of fertilizer to be used is 7 units per milliliter.

3. a) **Total Weight**

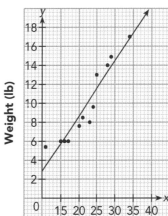

Diameter of Pumpkin (in.)

b) From the graphs, the weight of a pumpkin with a diameter of 24 inches is approximately 9 pounds.

c) No. Since the prediction is made based on the line of best fit, it is only an estimate. Not all pumpkins with a diameter of 24 inches will have the same weight.

2. a)

Amount of Fertilizer (units per mL)	0	1	2	3	4	5	6	7
Height at the End of the Month (in.)	2	2.5	4.5	5.1	6.5	8.2	11.6	14.8

Amount of Fertilizer (units per mL)	8	9	10	11	12	13	14
Height at the End of the Month (in.)	16	17.5	0	0	0	0	0

b) It appears that the plants died or did not grow at 11 when more than 9 units per milliliters of fertilizers were added.

4. a–b)

Altitude and Boiling of Water

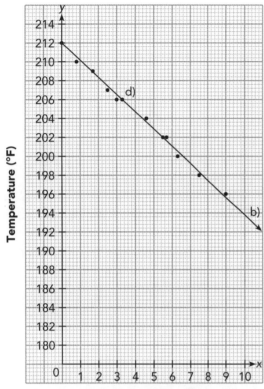

Height (ft. in 1,000)

The line of best fit passes through (0, 212) and (8, 197.2).

Slope $m = \dfrac{197.2 - 212}{8 - 0}$

$= -1.85$

The line passes the y-axis at the point (0, 212). So, the y-intercept, b, is 212.

The equation for the line of best fit is $y = -1.85x + 212$.

c) When $x = 3.2$, $y = -1.85(3.2) + 212$

$= 206.1$

The boiling point of water is 206.1°F.

d) When $y = 190$,

$y = -1.85x + 212$

$190 = -1.85x + 212$

$190 - 212 = -1.85x$

$-22 = -1.85x$

$\dfrac{-22}{-1.85} = \dfrac{-1.85x}{-1.85}$

$x \approx 11.9$

The altitude is 11,900 feet.

5. a)

Country

		Tokyo	Hong Kong	Total
Tour	**Economic**	90	41	131
	Standard	42	123	165
	Deluxe	18	36	54
	Total	150	200	350

b) 165 customers opted for the Standard package.

c) From the table, it appears that customers prefer the Standard package regardless of the location.

6. a)

Clothing Items Sold

		T–shirts	Pants	Shorts	Total
Day	**Monday**	12	5	18	35
	Tuesday	8	9	20	37
	Total	20	14	38	72

b) Let the wholesale cost of each pair of shorts be $x.

Total wholesale cost of T-shirts = $18 · 12

$= \$216$

Total wholesale cost of pants = $35 · 5

$= \$175$

Total wholesale cost of shorts = $x · 18

$= \$18x$

Total wholesale cost = $216 + $175 + $18x

$= \$(319 + 18x)$

Total sales from T-shirts = $23 · 12

$= \$276$

Total sales from pants = $48.50 · 5

$= \$242.50$

Total sales from shorts = $8.40 · 18

$= \$151.20$

Total sales = $276 + $242.50 + $151.20

$= \$669.70$

Profit = Total sales − Total wholesale cost

$\$152.70 = \$669.70 - \$(391 + 18x)$

$\$152.7 = \$278.7 - 18x$

$-126 = 18x$

$\dfrac{-126}{-18} = \dfrac{-18x}{-18}$

$x = \$7$

The wholesale cost of each pair of shorts is $7.

c)

Total Sales on Monday

Clothing Item	Wholesale Cost	Selling Price	Total Profit
T-Shirts	$216	$276	$60
Pants	$175	$242.50	$67.50
Shorts	$126	$151.20	$25.20
Total	$517	$669.70	$152.70

7. a)

Books

Titles	Fiction	Non-fiction	Reference Materials	Total
Adults	152	45	18	215
Children	160	40	27	227
Total	312	85	43	440

b) From the table, 227 children's titles and reference materials were sold by the end of the week.

c) The total number of adult and children fiction titles sold was 312.

d) $\frac{45}{215} = \frac{9}{43}$

$\frac{9}{43}$ of the adult titles sold are non-fiction.

8. a) Construct a two-way table for the weekly supply of seafood and vegetables:

Daily Supply

Supplier	Seafood	Vegetables	Total
A	82	51	133
B	50	47	97
Total	132	98	230

133 > 97; So, Supplier A supplied the greatest amount of food to the restaurant.

b) From the table in **a)**, the weekly supply of vegetables to the restaurant from both suppliers is 98 pounds.

c) $\frac{50}{132} = \frac{25}{66}$

$\frac{25}{66}$ of the weekly supply of seafood came from Supplier B.

d)

Daily Supply

Supplier	Seafood	Vegetables	Total
A	31	16	47
B	20	22	42
Total	51	38	89

Friday to Sunday

Supplier	Seafood	Vegetables	Total
A	51	35	86
B	30	25	55
Total	81	60	141

Supply of seafood from both suppliers during the weekdays = 51 lb

Supply of seafood from both suppliers during the weekend = 81 lb

Total weekly supply of seafood from both suppliers = 51 + 81
= 132 lb

Percent increase

$= \frac{81 - 51}{132} \cdot 100\%$

$= 22.7\%$

9. a) Number of girls taking a second language = 70% · 400
= 280

Number of girls taking German
$= \frac{1}{5} \cdot 280$
= 56

Number of girls taking French
= 280 − 56 − 100
= 124

Number of boys taking a second language = 400 − 280
= 120

Number of boys taking French $= \frac{1}{4} \cdot 120$
= 30

Number of boys taking German
= 120 − 30 − 36
= 54

Language

Gender	German	Spanish	French	Total
Girls	56	100	124	280
Boys	54	36	30	120
Total	110	136	154	400

b)

Language

Gender	German	Spanish	French	Total
Female	$\frac{56}{280} = 0.2$	$\frac{100}{280} \approx 0.36$	$\frac{124}{280} \approx 0.44$	1
Male	$\frac{54}{120} = 0.45$	$\frac{36}{120} = 0.3$	$\frac{30}{120} = 0.25$	1
Total	0.65	0.66	0.69	2

Among the girls, most of them prefer to take French as a second language, and the least of them prefer to take German as a second language. Among the boys, most of them prefer to take German as a second language, and the least of them prefer to take French as a second language.

c)

Language

Gender	German	Spanish	French	Total
Female	$\frac{56}{110} \approx 0.51$	$\frac{100}{136} \approx 0.74$	$\frac{124}{154} \approx 0.81$	2.06
Male	$\frac{54}{110} \approx 0.49$	$\frac{36}{136} \approx 0.26$	$\frac{30}{154} \approx 0.19$	0.94
Total	1	1	1	3

More girls take Spanish and French than boys. Among those who take German as their second language, it is almost evenly distributed between the boys and girls with slightly more girls.

10. a)

Year

Sport	2010	2011	2012	Total
Soccer	32	24	14	70
Basketball	16	14	8	38
Football	46	34	56	136
Total	94	72	78	244

b) Relative frequencies among the column:

Year

Sport	2010	2011	2012	Total
Soccer	$\frac{32}{94} \approx 0.34$	$\frac{24}{72} \approx 0.33$	$\frac{14}{78} \approx 0.18$	0.85
Basketball	$\frac{16}{94} \approx 0.17$	$\frac{14}{72} \approx 0.19$	$\frac{8}{78} \approx 0.10$	0.46
Football	$\frac{46}{94} \approx 0.49$	$\frac{34}{72} \approx 0.47$	$\frac{56}{78} \approx 0.72$	1.68
Total	1	1	1	3

In all the 3 years, football has the highest number of injuries; basketball has the least number of injuries.

Relative frequencies among the rows:

Year

Sport	2010	2011	2012	Total
Soccer	$\frac{32}{70} \approx 0.46$	$\frac{24}{70} \approx 0.34$	$\frac{14}{70} = 0.2$	1
Basketball	$\frac{16}{38} \approx 0.42$	$\frac{14}{38} \approx 0.37$	$\frac{8}{38} \approx 0.21$	1
Football	$\frac{46}{136} \approx 0.34$	$\frac{34}{136} \approx 0.25$	$\frac{56}{136} \approx 0.41$	1
Total	1.22	0.96	0.82	3

In both soccer and basketball, 2010 was the year that had the highest frequency of injuries occurring. In football, 2012 was the year that had the highest frequency of injuries.

11. Brain@Work

a)

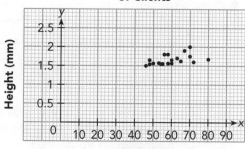

Mass and Height of Clients

The association between the person's mass and height is weak.

b)

Name	Alice	Sam	Kelvin	Patricia
Mass (kg)	50	76	70	65
Height (m)	1.56	2	1.78	1.63
BMI	20.5	19	22.1	24.5

Name	Owen	Bernice	Eunice	Ben
Mass (kg)	67	46	48	72
Height (m)	1.89	1.5	1.53	1.8
BMI	18.8	20.4	20.5	22.2

Name	Mike	Andrew	Ian	Janice
Mass (kg)	60	70	58	48
Height (m)	1.65	1.77	1.8	1.67
BMI	22.0	22.3	17.9	17.2

Name	June	Peter	Susan	Tom
Mass (kg)	53	80	55	63
Height (m)	1.58	1.68	1.56	1.7
BMI	21.2	28.3	22.6	21.8

Name	Roy	Amy	Nancy	Hillary
Mass (kg)	72	54	60	58
Height (m)	1.62	1.57	1.56	1.56
BMI	27.4	21.9	24.7	23.8

BMI

Gender	Within Healthy BMI Range	Not Within Healthy BMI Range	Total
Male	7	3	10
Female	9	1	10
Total	16	4	20

c)

BMI

Gender	Within Healthy BMI Range	Not Within Healthy BMI Range	Total
Male	$\frac{7}{16} \approx 0.44$	$\frac{3}{4} \approx 0.75$	1.19
Female	$\frac{9}{16} \approx 0.56$	$\frac{1}{4} \approx 0.25$	
Total	1	1	2

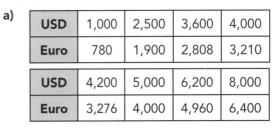

There are more females that fall within the healthy BMI range than males. So, there are more males not within the healthy BMI range.

12. Brain@Work

a)

USD	1,000	2,500	3,600	4,000
Euro	780	1,900	2,808	3,210

USD	4,200	5,000	6,200	8,000
Euro	3,276	4,000	4,960	6,400

b)

Euro and USD Exchange Rate

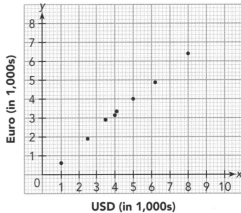

c) Because the graph is a straight line, it is a linear relationship.

Chapter 11

1. a)

Spinner 1

+	1	2	3	4	5
6	7	8	9	10	11
7	8	9	10	11	12
8	9	10	11	12	13
9	10	11	12	13	14
10	11	12	13	14	15

(left axis label: Spinner 2)

b)

Spinner 1

+	1	2	3	4	5
6	7	8	9	10	11
7	8	9	10	11	12
8	9	10	11	12	13
9	10	11	12	13	14
10	11	12	13	14	15

(left axis label: Spinner 2)

P(getting a sum of 10 or 12) = $\frac{8}{25}$

c)

Spinner 1

+	1	2	3	4	5
6	7	8	9	10	11
7	8	9	10	11	12
8	9	10	11	12	13
9	10	11	12	13	14
10	11	12	13	14	15

(left axis label: Spinner 2)

P(getting a sum of prime number) = $\frac{9}{25}$

2. a)

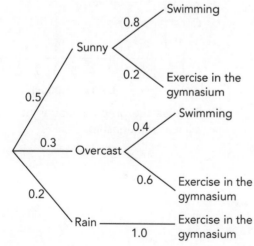

b) P(overcast, swimming)
= P(overcast) · P(swimming)
= 0.3(0.4)
= 0.12

c) P(exercise in the gymnasium)
= P(sunny, gymnasium) + P(overcast, gymnasium) + P(rain, gymnasium)
= 0.5(0.2) + 0.3(0.6) + 0.2(1.0)
= 0.1 + 0.18 + 0.2
= 0.48

3. a) P(egg, tuna) = $\frac{20}{70} \cdot \frac{30}{69}$

$= \frac{20}{161}$

b) P(ham, ham) = $\frac{18}{68} \cdot \frac{17}{67}$

$= \frac{9}{134}$

4. a) P(trapeze artist) = $\frac{5}{24}$

b) P(2 acrobats) = $\left(\frac{16}{24}\right)\left(\frac{15}{23}\right)\left(\frac{8}{22}\right) \cdot 3$

$= \frac{120}{253}$

c) P(not ringmaster) = 1 − P(ringmaster)

$= 1 - \frac{1}{24} \cdot 3$

$= \frac{7}{8}$

5. a) Out of the 5 days, the possible ways of her taking bus to school on exactly 3 days are: Day (1, 2, 3); (1, 2, 4); (1, 2, 5); (1, 3, 4); (1, 3, 5); (1, 4, 5); (2, 3, 4); (2, 3, 5); (2, 4, 5) and (3, 4, 5)
P(taking bus on exactly 3 days out of 5 days)
= 10(0.77)(0.77)(0.77)(0.23)(0.23)
≈ 0.242

b) Out of the 5 days, the possible ways of her taking bus to school on 3 consecutive days are:
Day (1, 2, 3); (2, 3, 4) and (3, 4, 5)
P(taking bus on 3 consecutive days out of 5 days)
= 3(0.77)(0.77)(0.77)(0.23)(0.23)
≈ 0.0725

6. a) Total number of books available in the school library
$$= 40 + 20 + 35 + 45 + 15 + 10$$
$$= 165$$
Number of fiction books $= 40 + 20 + 35$
$$= 95$$
$$P(\text{two fiction books}) = \frac{95}{165} \cdot \frac{94}{164}$$
$$= \frac{893}{2706}$$

b) $P(\text{magazine, comic}) = \frac{15}{165} \cdot \frac{10}{164}$
$$= \frac{5}{902}$$
$$= 0.00554$$
$$P(\text{romance, thriller}) = \frac{20}{165} \cdot \frac{40}{164}$$
$$= \frac{40}{1353}$$
$$\approx 0.0296$$
Since P(romance, thriller) > P(magazine, comic), it is more likely that she borrows both a romance and a thriller.

7. a)

First Meeting

Second Meeting	Mon	Tue	Wed	Thurs	Fri	Sat	Sun
Tue	(M, T)						
Wed	(M, W)	(T, W)					
Thurs	(M, Th)	(T, Th)	(W, Th)				
Fri	(M, F)	(T, F)	(W, F)	(Th, F)			
Sat	(M, Sa)	(T, Sa)	(W, Sa)	(Th, Sa)	(F, Sa)		
Sun	(M, Su)	(T, Su)	(W, Su)	(Th, Su)	(F, Su)	(Sa, Su)	

$$P(\text{Mon, Tue}) = \frac{1}{21}$$

b)

First Meeting

Second Meeting	Mon	Tue	Wed	Thurs	Fri	Sat	Sun
Tue	(M, T)						
Wed	(M, W)	(T, W)					
Thurs	(M, Th)	(T, Th)	(W, Th)				
Fri	(M, F)	(T, F)	(W, F)	(Th, F)			
Sat	(M, Sa)	(T, Sa)	(W, Sa)	(Th, Sa)	(F, Sa)		
Sun	(M, Su)	(T, Su)	(W, Su)	(Th, Su)	(F, Su)	(Sa, Su)	

$$P(\text{not on Mon and Tues but on Wed}) = \frac{4}{21}$$

8. a) Since no two dresses are the same
P(same dress) = 0

b) Total number of dresses
$$= 10 + 4 + 2 + 3 + 2 + 2 = 23$$
Number of dresses excluding orange dresses $= 23 - 4 = 19$
P(5 non orange dresses)
$$= \frac{19}{23} \cdot \frac{18}{22} \cdot \frac{17}{21} \cdot \frac{16}{20} \cdot \frac{15}{19}$$
$$= \frac{612}{1771}$$
$$\approx 0.346$$

9. a) P(James get to spin the wheel)
= P(Charles gets a number less than 5) ·
P(Stacey gets a number less than 5)
$$= \frac{4}{6} \cdot \frac{4}{6}$$
$$= \frac{4}{9}$$

b) P(James not winning a prize)
= P(James gets a number less than 4)
+ P(James gets a number greater than 4 and lands on "black hole")
$$= \frac{3}{6} + \frac{2}{6} \cdot \frac{3}{25}$$
$$= \frac{27}{50}$$

10. a) $P(\text{wake up on time}) = \frac{9}{20}$
$$1 - a = \frac{9}{20}$$
$$1 - a - 1 = \frac{9}{20} - 1$$
$$-a = -\frac{11}{20}$$
$$a = \frac{11}{20}$$
$$b = 1 - \frac{2}{3}$$
$$= \frac{1}{3}$$

b) P(punctual) = P(wake up late, punctual)
+ P(wake up on time, punctual)
$$= \frac{1}{4} \cdot \frac{1}{3} + \frac{3}{4} \cdot \frac{3}{5}$$
$$= \frac{8}{15}$$
$$P(\text{late}) = 1 - \frac{8}{15}$$
$$= \frac{7}{15}$$
Since P(punctual) > P(late), she is more likely to be punctual on any given day.

Brain@Work

11. a)

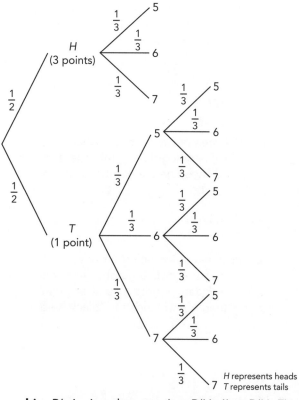

H represents heads
T represents tails

b) P(winning the game) = P(H, 6) + P(H, 7)

$$= \frac{1}{2} \cdot \frac{1}{3} + \frac{1}{2} \cdot \frac{1}{3}$$

$$= \frac{1}{3}$$

c) P(getting a sum of 9 or 12)

= P(H, 6) + P(T, 5, 6) + P(T, 6, 5)

$$= \frac{1}{2} \cdot \frac{1}{3} + \frac{1}{2} \cdot \frac{1}{3} \cdot \frac{1}{3} + \frac{1}{2} \cdot \frac{1}{3} \cdot \frac{1}{3}$$

$$= \frac{5}{18}$$

Brain@Work

12. a)

Route	Probability of Being Congested	Probability of Not Being Congested
Office – Sixth Avenue	0.2	0.8
Sixth Avenue – East Park	0.55	0.45
East Park – Home	0.6	0.4
Office – City Center	0.7	0.3
City Center – Home	0.2	0.8
Office – North Bridge Highway	0.6	0.4
North Bridge Highway – Home	0.45	0.55

b) P(route 1) = 0.8(0.45)(0.4)
          = 0.144

P(route 2) = 0.3(0.8)
          = 0.24

P(route 3) = 0.4(0.55)
          = 0.22

Since P(route 2) > P(route 3) > P(route 1); the route that she is most likely to take is route 2.

BLANK

BLANK